The Sigma Male Bible

DISCOVER THE RULES TO BE INDEPENDENT, CONFIDENT, SELF-SUFFICIENT, AND STRONG ENOUGH TO BE AN ALPHA MALE. UNLEASH THE LONE WOLF WITHIN AND ACHIEVE IMMENSE LEVELS OF SUCCESS

Table of Contents

Introduction 2

Chapter 1: The Sigma Male Grindset 5

Chapter 2: Everything Begins with You..................... 25

Chapter 3: The Sigma Male and His Success Mindset...104

Chapter 4: Hypnosis, Empathy, and Psychic Abilities..120

Chapter 5: Body Language for Strategic Communication147

Chapter 6: The Sigma Male and Fashion 167

Chapter 7: The Principle of Self-Multiplication 185

Chapter 8: The Sigma Male and His Romantic Conquests193

Chapter 9: Corporate and Career Dominance.................. 204

Chapter 10: The Sigma Male's Spirituality 213

Conclusion.. 220

Introduction

Everyone loves a confident man! Okay, that may be a bit of a stretch.

Everyone loves a confident, self-sufficient, and compassionate man who understands how to treat everyone around him with respect but still has a way of making sure he is well respected by the people in his world. When you meet men like this, you are instantly drawn to them. The ladies love to be with them. The men want to be like them. Their bosses at work respect them. Their contemporaries defer to them. Even when they hide under the veil of 'not being interested in the spotlight,' leadership and positions of responsibility always have a way of falling back to them.

As you read through the pages of this book, you will recall a number of men who fall into this category that you have met at some point in your life. This could be at work, in the neighborhood, while dropping off your child (or niece) at school, or even while jogging around the neighborhood on an early Saturday morning.

You may not be able to tell what it is, but something about this type of man draws you in immediately. Regardless of how hard you may try to fight it, you may not be able to shake the thoughts of this man away from your mind for the rest of the day. Even in his silence, everything about him screams "poise, class, and being in absolute control of the world around him."

Being this man comes with its perks. We have already hinted at the fact that everyone tends to look to him for leadership and to get the job done. However, this isn't the only advantage that comes from being that guy. When you become this guy we have started describing (and would continue to describe in subsequent chapters of this book), you'd discover that life automatically becomes easier for you.

Your romantic life will become way better than before because the ladies now tend to flock towards you (as opposed to the time when you had to do all you could to woo a lady who may end up revealing she isn't interested in pursuing anything with you). In addition, your career and business will become much better because you now understand yourself, know your strengths and weaknesses, and have developed a self-management plan to ensure that you are always at your A-game regardless of the obvious challenges life may throw in your face at every point.

In a nutshell, the persona of a Sigma Male is a representation of what it means to be a truly successful man in the 21st century.

As a Sigma Male, you are 100% in control of your life, and the results your life produces are exactly what you want. You are productive, goal-oriented, wealthy, successful with an incredible sense of style, and you have developed the uncanny ability to get just any girl you want.

Do you know what the best part is?

Sigma men aren't just born.

No one is born with all the abilities we have discussed. Sigma males are made. Over time, they subject themselves to be trained, mentored, and they take their personal development/the acquisition of powerful habits seriously. These are responsible for the perfect male figures you see, respect, and so want to be like.

This, on the other hand, is good news already. It simply means that regardless of where you are at right now, you can take responsibility for your life and decide that you want to move from dangling at the bottom of the food chain to becoming the perfect sigma male who would love his life, enjoy the benefits that come with being a powerful male figure in every figure, and also serve as a massive inspiration for someone tomorrow.

Take a second to think about the millions of boys you can empower by inspiring them to let go of their inhibitions and reach out to become the powerful men that they have always wanted to be.

It sounds amazing, right?

Are you ready to get started on that journey of self-discovery and transformation from a mediocre man to a powerful sigma male? Let's get started immediately.

Chapter 1: The Sigma Male Grindset

Overview of the Concept

Many things come to mind when people hear the term 'sigma male.' For some people, a sigma male is one who has mastered the art of being in control of everything around him. For these people, when the words are mentioned, they have the picture of a burly man in his late fifties, sitting on a reclining chair and smoking his pipe in the setting sun.

On the other hand, some other people think of the sigma male as the overbearing, rude young man at work, who was recently promoted to become the boss of everyone else, and who doesn't understand the first thing about empathy, emotional intelligence, and who looks down on everyone else over the bridge of his nose.

Well, both pictures are wrong.

While a sigma male can easily be a burly silver fox who is beginning to get into the later stage of his life and also a young man who was recently promoted to being a boss at work, neither of these factors makes a sigma male, and this is because a sigma male is fashioned by what's inside him and not just his age, body structure, or his position at work. Some of the sigma males you would meet in your life will be incredibly lean, while others will be burly and ripped. Some will be bosses at work, while others will be effective employees and powerful team players.

This is why it is important that you open yourself up to clearly understand the concept of the sigma male and what it is all about. This chapter will shed more light on who a sigma male is and why you should start channeling your energies into becoming one.

Who is a Sigma Male?

Heads-up.

Throughout this book, you may stumble across places where the words "lone wolf" have been used. Don't get too excited and begin wondering what the word means and how it relates to the conversation at hand. Simply put, the lone wolf is another name for the term "sigma male."

Now that we have that out of the way, "sigma male" is a term that is used to describe the societally perfect and acceptable picture of a man. A sigma male is a man who is popular, successful, influential, self-reliant, and super independent. At first, the term was used as part of a system of categorizing men in ways that they presented in society.

Going by this structure, there were the Alpha males (the independent ones who were considered the leaders of the pack), the Beta males (who were more skilled at managing resources and ensuring that the pack was well taken care of), and the Omega males (who were more or less considered to be effeminate and in need of protection by the Alpha males).

Over time, however, the definition and use of the term "Sigma male" has evolved as it is a term that many men now want to be associated with - because it speaks of beauty, valor, and the dignity of a man.

When examined from a different angle, the sigma male is one who refuses to play their games by the socially acceptable standards but who still manages to win every time. At first glance, the sigma male may not look like much. He may not:

- Be strong and burly, but he somehow manages to get through life even though he looks like he would need help from time to time (remember, we already hinted that you don't need to hit the gym and bulk up like The Rock - the famous wrestler - to be a sigma male, right)?

- Be classically handsome but exudes some kind of inexplicable charm that makes the women (and even men) fall over themselves to be with him.
- Have a very good fashion sense, but he has a way of pulling off every outfit he wears that he becomes the trend wherever he is. The sigma male is one person who can wear whatever he chooses without giving much thought to conventional dress principles for men but still manages to look dapper.
- Be the most visible at work, but he is liked by his bosses and would most likely be the first (or among the first) to be promoted whenever these opportunities come by.

In short, the sigma male is an enigma, one that many people (and scientists alike) have devoted their lives to trying to understand how he lives and what makes him get the kinds of results he gets. He is successful and popular, but at the same time, he is rebellious and prefers to live life on his own terms, not conforming to the dictates of the general society.

The Origin of the Sigma Male Grindset

The sigma male grindset simply refers to the mindset possessed by the male who sits at the top of the societal hierarchy (that is, the sigma male). It is the combination of everything that makes the sigma male who he is; the mindset he has toward work, his dedication and passion for seeing his life change, his commitment to excellence, his love for himself and dignity, his mastery of his strengths and weaknesses, and his cutting-edge approach to matters of the heart.

The Sigma Male Grindset was extricated from a more common term, "rise and grind," which is more or less the sigma male's note to self; his commitment to keep moving on regardless of what life brings to him.

The sigma male theory was first proposed by Vox Day as part of the overarching socio-sexual hierarchy of males in which they tried to critically examine all males and define exactly where each of them fit into the socio-sexual pole. The concept of socio-sexuality is one that simply teaches that as far as society is concerned, all men are not the same. According to this placement, the men who were at the top of the ladder were more likely to be more successful, wealthier, and even have access to the best women for lasting relationships. Those at the base of the chain, on the other hand, had to walk through life like they had nothing else (because they actually didn't). All they had to do was pray that the overdogs find them worthy of anything at all so that they have to scrounge for the leftovers in every sense of the word.

According to this placement, there were originally 6 categories of men:

1. An Alpha male
2. Beta male
3. Gamma male

4. Delta male
5. Omega male
6. Lambda male

While this categorization made sense at first, history showed that it was impossible to think of this as perfect. This is because, over time, there seemed to be a class of men who never did life like everyone thought they would. The shocker was that when you thought they would crash down to the end of their lives, they had a way of pulling through and shooting to the limelight.

Leonardo Da Vinci was one of such men.

As a result of the gaps that started appearing when people began to question the potency of this classification, there was a need to revise it a little, and this is where the concept of the sigma male fully came into play. The expansion of the socio-sexual spectrum was great, but it was not without its own challenges.

For one, alpha males began to feel threatened. For a long time, they had been at the highest rung of the ladder, enjoying their lives, living on their own terms, getting the best women, and enjoying power/affluence. Why bring in another category of men to sit alongside them on the hierarchy of things?

This began the cold war between Alphas and Sigma males. In many accounts, the sigma male is considered to be on the same hierarchical level as the alpha male, although they choose to sit outside the spectrum by choice. Every other male on the spectrum seems to fall in place by themselves because they already do not have a lot to prove. The alpha males, on the other hand, tend to clash with the sigma males almost every time. Considering that alpha males love to be deferred to, they get irritated when they have to deal with the regular sigma male who has absolutely no intentions of doing so. In many cases, the alpha male would have to spar with the sigma male in another way that may not be physical.

This can be in a public show of brilliance.

And because the sigma males are generally smarter than the alpha males (who mostly rely on their brawn and physical charm to get their way), history has it that alpha males are mostly embarrassed when they have to meet sigma males who end up making a public show out of them.

Throughout the ages, the concept of the sigma male has continued to grow and spread across the world. Who wouldn't love to be that man who rises to the position of authority and influence regardless of the stones that life threw their way?

Over time, many authors and experts have postulated concepts that can help just anyone to take control of their lives and become the sigma male in his world. Simply applying the strategies communicated in this book and being consistent at doing them right will turn you from whatever you may be at the moment to becoming the sigma male who has everything under control.

Essential Qualities of the Sigma Male

By this time, you may be asking yourself what the heck is all the fuss about being a sigma male and why it feels like everyone is interested in becoming one. The thing is that if you want to have a shot at becoming that successful man you have always envisioned yourself to be, and you do not have the luxury of being an alpha male (or being blessed with the personality that is outgoing and charismatic), becoming a sigma male is your next best bet.

Here are the basic qualities of the sigma male. This is why everyone wants to be a sigma male (and even why you may want to consider becoming one yourself).

They are Mostly Loners

Please get this straight from the start. The fact that we say that sigma males tend to be loners doesn't mean that they dislike the company of people or that they are extremely introverted. It simply means that the sigma male is confident enough to be all by himself and thrive well without the company of others.

Despite these, they can be lovely when they are with people in public. Their ability to put their best feet forward makes them easily likable. In addition, when a sigma male likes and feels comfortable around you, they don't mind opening up and allowing you to see their deepest sides.

They Can Lead Even Without Being in Positions of Authority

One of the major attributes that make the sigma male completely different from the alpha male is that they have the understanding that they do not have to be at the helm of affairs to lead and enforce change from wherever they are.

As a result, it is not unusual to see a sigma male making a ton of difference at work, in the neighborhood, in church, or in society - even without being known as a leader of sorts. The sigma male prefers to lead by example and mutual consent and doesn't take pride in enforcing their dominance over people.

They may not even believe that they are dominant in the first place.

They are Remarkable Listeners

This could be directly traceable to their abilities to feel what the people around them are feeling every time. Because they understand the value of mutual respect, the sigma male would rather keep quiet and respect whoever they are interacting with when the time for a conversation comes.

This is another skill that makes them generally endearing.

They Don't Rely on Societal Constructs to Decide Their Fate

One endearing quality of the sigma male is that they understand the value of taking their lives into their hands and that they are completely responsible for the outcome of their lives.

As opposed to the alpha male who does well when he is in a competitive environment and can establish his dominance over every other person or the beta male who prefers to work/thrive in a stress-free environment, the sigma male becomes his own inspiration and dials down any other competitors when the needs arise.

This is one of the major reasons why it is agreed that the sigma male does life on his terms and is most likely to succeed regardless of where he finds himself.

Small But Closely-Knit Social Circles

If there's one thing you should have gleaned from all that has been said so far about the sigma male, it should be that they prefer minimal drama in their lives. As a result, you would most likely see the sigma male in a small but closely-knit circle.

Since they never feel pushed to impress people, the sigma male may not be considered a 'social butterfly' and would rather stick to a few people he knows and completely trusts. However, getting into that circle isn't a walk in the park as the sigma male prioritizes loyalty and expects it of everyone around them.

A Sigma Male is a Loyal Person

Considering that they prioritize a small and closely-knit circle (and their penchant for prequalifying their friends and close associates), the sigma male is characterized by loyalty.

When a sigma male tells you that he has your back, rest assured that you can take that to the bank.

The Sigma Male isn't Scared of Taking Risks

And this is one other thing that makes them successful overall. The sigma male sets his mind on a price, pursues it with singleness of mind, and isn't ashamed of being seen as silly or crazy.

Then again, since they are more likely to create a path for themselves, the sigma male is blessed with a strong will and a clear understanding of what they must do to get to where they have to be in the future. They do the craziest things and walk out the door with huge smirks on their faces.

They Can Easily Step Up and Save the Day

Regardless of the fact that they are hardly ever obsessed with being in the spotlight, a sigma male may not have any challenges with stepping up and becoming the leader that any organization and pack needs. Considering that they are skilled at being a number of persons at the same time, the sigma male only needs to master the art of harnessing the inner alpha, and he would make a good enough dominant leader any day, any time.

Humble

The sigma male is generally perceived as humbler than an alpha male. This is because they aren't focused on praises, public admiration, and making people remember that they are the ones that call the shots. Instead, they are more interested in getting the job done and being efficient in every sense of the word.

Considering these, sigma males are considered to be less self-indulgent and humble. They seek the greater good and would be happier when the needs of the overarching group are met. The perception that they are humble is because of their ability to let their personal gains go and focus on achieving a set goal.

They aren't Exactly Social

Another thing you would notice about a sigma male is that they aren't the definition of social butterflies. When you step into a social function, you may find the sigma male all by himself, nursing a drink in the corner of the booth. However, they easily compensate for this with their ability to be endearing.

So, even though you may not see them flying around with people, when you take a closer look, you would see that people are drawn toward them like they are a black hole.

Charisma

Everything we have said about the sigma male so far bleeds into one overarching word; a sigma male is mostly a charismatic man. They know what to say, how and when to say it, and they understand the most effective ways to communicate.

The sigma male is skilled at carrying himself with an air of confidence. Coupled with a sense of importance and a dedication to getting results, the sigma male is known for being charismatic.

In addition, the sigma male is also self-secure and doesn't rely on external validation to know and be reminded of what he is worth.

The Sigma Male Loves Having New Experiences

This attribute can sometimes make him come off as a drifter. However, it is important to note that sigma males are known for traveling and solo activities, and they would do anything to try out new things and visit new places.

Defiant in the Face of Bullying

When the sigma male is pitted against an alpha (like in a corporate setting or an encounter that demands that they push for a romantic relationship with someone both of them are interested in), he tends to become defiant.

The sigma male, by default, hates the ideas of societal constructs and prefers to be alone. This tendency is fanned and becomes worse when he encounters an alpha male who seeks to place him under duress. The sigma male doesn't mind getting into a fight with the alpha, rather than just bending to the alpha's will without giving much consideration to himself.

In summary, the sigma male is a fighter.

Clear Signs that You are Becoming a Sigma Male

Take a while to pore over the points we will be discussing in this section of the book. If you fit the description of the man we are about to make, it suggests that you are already on your way to becoming a successful sigma male. If that isn't the case with you, don't lose hope because, as we have already discussed, just anyone can develop the skills required to become a sigma male.

You Have a Rebellious Streak

And this is not the type that makes you want to pull out a machete and hack people to pieces when something is demanded of you. Instead, it is the inability to be put within the confines of a box or to be caged by societal construct.

It may even show up as the inability to take no for an answer.

If you have had a history of feeling yourself refuse to fit into a predetermined social construct, it could be a sign that you are already on your way to becoming a sigma male.

You Believe Strongly in Your Ideas and that You Can Succeed on Your Terms

We are all taught that success comes in a specific way and that to be successful, you have to figure out what successors have done and define your most profitable path to doing the same. This theory works for everyone else, except the sigma male.

One of the first things you would notice as a sigma male is a strong belief that you can succeed all by yourself and by following a pathway that would most times be novel and unique to your life's journey. You are least concerned by what people think and would rather focus on understanding your purpose, getting the hang of your core values, and working your way to becoming a poster example of the man you have always envisioned yourself to end up as.

As a sigma male, you strongly believe that you can do life on your own terms. And the truth is, if you follow the pathway we'll cover in his book, you should be able to.

You Prefer the Silence of Your Own Company

If you are presented with two choices:

A. Go out with the boys for a fun evening out. Nothing much; just spend time with them over a few drinks in an active club, and
B. Spend your night indoors, maybe with a plate of your best meal and Netflix, or poring over some documents (that is, getting some work done).

The normal guy in you would want to choose the first option. However, the sigma male in you would most likely end up staying back. Most times, sigma males have to be dragged out of their homes by their group of close friends. If this doesn't happen, the average sigma male would rather stay indoors and maximize their quiet time (or at least indulge themselves with their imagination of what success looks and feels like).

You Adapt Easily to Change

Say you get to work tomorrow and discover that without giving you a heads-up, they have placed a new boss to head your department; one thing you would notice is that you wouldn't spend time bickering over the sudden change.

In fact, don't be surprised if (as a sigma male) you hear the message once and move on to continue with the work allocated to you as though nothing happened just a few minutes later. While other colleagues may have a hard time wrapping their heads around these sudden changes, you may not even be able to understand the reason why they're freaking out.

Sigma males are generally more malleable (when compared to alpha males) and, as a result, do not have a hard time fitting into any circle they find themselves in.

Equity is Your Watchword

As a sigma male, you can't easily wrap your head around the idea that people should be treated differently based on some societal constructs. As a result of this, you would find it easier to engage with people from all walks of life because you are doing this out of genuine curiosity and not just because you are looking for some kind of favor in return.

Considering your pure intentions, you believe in treating everyone with mutual respect, knowing fully well that humans are humans and not to be used as a means to your ends.

You are Mostly Self-Reliant

As a sigma male, you tend to first introspect when you encounter challenges. Your slogan is "the answer lies within," and you would rather spend time in a contemplative mood (seeking solutions to your challenges, not just mulling over them and wondering why your life is difficult) rather than run around looking for solutions.

The sigma male would only open up to the people closest to him when he has a challenge, and that is when he knows that he has exhausted his options as an individual and understands that it is time to take things a step further.

People Have Described You as Being an Enigma

If you have ever heard the people in your world describing you as an 'enigma' or you have caught them staring at you with a perplexed look on their faces, then it is quite possible that you fit the description of the sigma male.

One thing the people around you agree on is that your life is strange. You do not look as serious as they expect you to be, but somehow, you always end up successful and the chosen one.

Reasons Why You Should Start Considering Becoming a Sigma Male

As you must have seen by now, being a sigma male comes with its perks - many of them, at that. One of the major perks of being a sigma male is that you call the shots of your life. You decide the path you want to walk, deal with the consequences of being rejected (although you are mostly unphased with the opinions of others), and against all odds, you move on to become a successful man in your field of interest.

In addition, the sigma male is blessed to be the man who makes a massive change in his world. If you take a look at most of the sensational men who have lived before now (and whose stories have been preserved over time), you will discover one thing about them. Most of them were sigma males. If you intend to do big things with your life, this is one path you should strongly consider walking down.

Nothing gives you control over your life, like being able to call the shots and not waiting on other people to make things work for you. Then again, the world is hardly an ideal place, so you would have to figure out exactly how to make things work for you, even when the odds are heavily stacked up against you. This, in a nutshell, is the life the sigma male lives.

Chapter Summary

1. The sigma male is one who is characterized by his uncanny ability to chart his path through life, live on his own terms, and still become successful - even against all odds.
2. Usually, the sigma male has to live without the scope of societal constructs and social ladders. He doesn't like being held back by what people think about him, as he would rather walk his novel path to success with dignity.
3. Alpha males are mostly threatened by the presence of sigma males in their circles. This is because sigma males do not follow any predictable social strata but somehow manage to gain and hold the respect and attention of every other person they come in contact with. Then again, considering their ability to be malleable, a sigma male can do well and hit his targets regardless of the obvious challenges he may be facing at every instance.
4. There are standard characteristics that show that you are a sigma male or that you are already well on your way to becoming one. We discussed 7 of them in this chapter. Suppose those attributes describe your life at the moment; congratulations because you are already on the right path. If they don't describe your life, on the other hand, there's still nothing to be afraid of because we already mentioned that you could learn/perfect the art of becoming a sigma male.

Chapter 2: Everything Begins with You

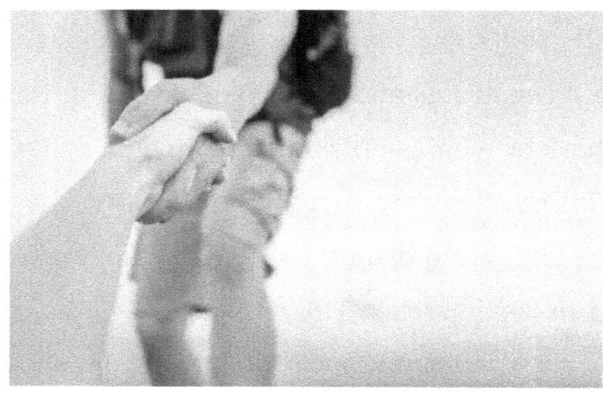

Have you taken out time to study the way athletes are trained? If you have, you won't find the saying, "It all begins with you," strange or new.

The athlete who ends up winning a major medal per season (like in the Olympics) spends their lives and previous years training for the main event. Although he would only compete for a day (or a few days at best), he hits the gym every day, runs a few laps around the entire court every day, and listens to a griping coach even when all he wants to do is bench press the silence into him.

One thing that has stood out for these guys is their understanding of who they are. Before getting started on their journey in any sport of choice, top athletes spend time on self-discovery. They take a look at their body structure, the advantages and disadvantages they have by being born a certain way, and they also take a while to understand the nitty-gritty of the sport they want to venture into.

One thing you would see these successful athletes doing all their lives is studying. They pore over the successes of their predecessors in hopes that they can find clues to become the best at their field of interest (because success leaves clues, right)? They also analyze their opponents (in cases of combative sports like wrestling and boxing games) with hopes that they can unearth patterns and discover their opponent's Achilles heel.

They do these for months and years, and when the time comes, they walk gallantly on stage. They perform flawlessly and walk off stage amid deafening cheers and the trophy they had their eyes on from the beginning. Although it is easy to take a snapshot of time (the moment they were winning and being cheered by millions of people), these athletes never forget one thing for the rest of their lives, and that's...

Everything begins with you!

If the athlete isn't careful enough to take a critical look at himself and understand what his advantages and disadvantages are (so he can play to his strengths and lose his weaknesses), or if he doesn't study his predecessors and competitors, he will walk upstage only to be disappointed when he gets beaten and publicly disgraced.

Dear sigma male, please take a cue from the athlete as we begin your journey into a new you. Everything you seek to become and have all begins with you. The money, fame, influence, impact, and every other thing in-between all begin with you. If you don't understand that you have a primary assignment to reinvent yourself and become the man who is deserving of all the things you want, you may end up leading your entire life trying to get something that never comes to you.

In this chapter, we will help you start your journey toward a better understanding of "you." In this chapter, we will take a deep dive into your mind and help you get started on your journey to self-actualization.

The Four Pillars of a Sigma Male's Personality

When you dissect a sigma male (okay, don't think gray thoughts. You don't have to place him on a dissecting table and cut his skin open. You just need to pay closer attention to him and spend time in his world), you will notice that there are 4 major aspects of his life that make up his overarching "personality."

First off, let us take a quick look at the meaning of the word personality.

Your personality is simply all the independent factors that coagulate to make you who you are. Wikipedia defines it as the characteristic set of behaviors, cognitions, and emotional patterns that evolve from biological and environmental factors, amongst others. Furthermore, your personality refers to the set of basic thoughts and action patterns you display throughout your life which are responsible for your uniqueness.

The sigma male's personality is simply the body of traits he possesses that make him an enigmatic and successful man.

When you interact with a sigma male over time, you will discover that all attributes he displays throughout the course of his life are hinged on 4 cardinal pillars. These are:

1. Mental Strength
2. Physical Allure/Appearance
3. Emotional Intelligence
4. Needs Mastery

It is important to point out that if you can become a master at all these pillars, you will be unrivaled in every sense of the word. Although we will be taking a closer look at all these points in subsequent chapters (plus what you must do to become a master of all of them), here's a quick introduction to these pillars.

Mental Strength

Considering all the hurdles you would be encountering on your journey to becoming a powerful sigma male (plus the rejection you would get from the people in your life), if you aren't mentally strong, you may find yourself faltering along the way.

Mental strength is simply a more 'fashionable' name for mental toughness. You need to be tough because if you aren't, you will get sidetracked and begin to feel the need to conform to societal norms.

Remember that, as a sigma male, you have very little business with conforming to these norms.

Physical Allure

People see you before they engage in a conversation with you. As a result, they may make assumptions about you based on what you look like. The age-long saying that "you are addressed the way you dress" isn't a cliche for lousy schoolboys who can't tell the difference between their left and right hands. It holds true now more than ever, especially if you want to grab and hold the attention of your dream woman.

You must master the art of being physically enchanting/alluring.

Yes. Those concepts aren't for women alone.

Emotional Intelligence

This is a measure of how well you understand your feelings and the feelings of the people around you. Emotional intelligence entails being able to identify and effectively manage the feelings of everyone in every situation.

Emotional intelligence is a skill that every powerful leader possesses, and if you intend to become a remarkable sigma male, you have to come to terms with the fact that you need a trailer-load of emotional intelligence to navigate the world of men.

Needs Mastery

"You mustn't always indulge yourself!"

This is probably one of the loudest warnings you would hear if you were to tear open the minds of every successful and remarkable sigma male. The type of life sigma males live (and the heights they have to attain in their lives) demands that they master the art of selective indulgence. Then again, needs mastery demands that you also master the game of delayed gratification.

Your finances, health, relationships, and every other area of your life require you to take a pause and master the art of self-control (needs mastery).

On this happy note, let's dive into the concepts that serve as the foundation for an exceptional life of the sigma male.

The Foundational Concepts of Personal Dominance

Personal dominance is the basis of everything you would achieve as a sigma male. Simply put, self/personal dominance is the art of mastering your body and emotions to such an extent that you dictate the direction your body moves, and not the other way round.

Personal dominance is an overarching phenomenon that covers the concepts we will be exploring in this chapter.

Self-Motivation

If you set goals, you would agree that one of the things that follow after achieving a goal is a sense of emotional high.

When you sit down with a pen and paper, take a peek into the future and lay down strategic plans to get you to a place you want to be (in life, your career, your business, or even with your relationships). You would feel a sense of direction and even the emotional push needed to get you to where you would like to be.

This could also come to you after you have attended an event and been pummeled with a lot of motivational speeches.

While these are great, you may be faced with one challenge. When the rubber hits the road, you may start working on the goals you set only to find yourself in a bind a few days later. Usually, whenever you start working on your goals, there will be days when you don't feel like getting out of bed. There would be Mondays when you wake up and wish you had the power to flick your fingers and bring everyone back to the previous Friday. Many times, all the motivational videos on YouTube won't give you the emotional boost you need, and more often than not, you would be tempted to let go of all the lofty goals you set for yourself and crawl back under the duvet.

At these times, the foundational concept of personal dominance you need to bring into play is the concept of self-motivation.

Self-motivation is one's ability to draw inspiration from themselves. Simply put, it is the internal state that allows you to initiate and sustain desirable actions while exerting yourself to stop the unneeded actions as well. A clear example of self-motivation playing out is when you come back from work at the end of a stressful day. You enter your house exhausted, hungry, and in need of getting refreshed.

Even without consulting anyone, you walk into the kitchen, fix something to eat, get your stomach filled, draw a bath, and freshen up.

If you didn't have self-motivation at work here, you wouldn't have been able to get these done. Without self-motivation, you may find yourself sitting down on the couch and mindlessly surfing through the channels on TV, waiting for someone else to get you off the couch and into the kitchen or bathroom.

One of the superpowers every sigma male possesses is the ability to motivate himself. Even without waiting for anyone to chaperone him, the sigma male understands that every other person is busy going about their daily lives and that if he stays seated every day, waiting for help (and motivation) to come from without, he won't get anywhere with his life.

While it is okay and even important to consume a lot of motivational content, self-motivation is one of the best gifts you can give yourself as a sigma male who wants to shatter glass ceilings and do remarkable things with his life. In the next sections of this chapter, we will explore the importance of self-motivation and how you can get started on your journey to becoming the sigma male who abounds in self-motivation.

Why is Self-Motivation Important to the Sigma Male?

Here are some reasons why you must have an ever-increasing supply of self-motivation as a sigma male.

1. **The World is Busy**

This may be one of the most painful things you may read today, but it is a truth that begs to be said, nonetheless. While you may want to build sandcastles in the sky by believing that there's someone out there who would place their entire lives on hold to make sure that you get everything you want in life, the hard and honest truth is that people have more important things to think of and be worried about.

The average person you would meet in life is obsessed with how to make their own lives better. They are thinking about the things they must do to hit their next goal and how to ensure that they become better people than they were just a few weeks ago.

With this in mind, you have a responsibility (at least to yourself) to ensure that you are doing the same. While people are busy thinking about how they can make their lives better, ensure you are worried about the same thing; how to crush your next goal and become the self-sufficient man you have been called to be.

2. Sometimes, External Motivation Isn't Handy

There are some days when you would wake up, and you wouldn't be in the mood for anything, not even to reach out to your phone and play your favorite motivational speech (or even ask Siri to search out the trending motivational video online and play it for you). When these days come, you will have to rely solely on your abilities to be self-motivated if you stand any chances of sticking to the plan and achieving everything you intend to.

Everyone thinks motivation is free and easy to reach. Well, that's true until it isn't.

3. It Ensures You Break Out of Bad Cycles on Time

We already discussed that one of the things self-motivation does for you is that it helps you to be brutally honest with yourself. When this is the case, you are able to identify terrible habits in your life, take the necessary steps needed to change them, and thereby enforce permanent change in your life in that regard.

In the later chapters of this book, we will be looking at habit formation and how habits affect the overall life of the sigma male.

However, it is important to note that high-performing sigma males aren't emotionally attached to anything that doesn't give them the results they need. If they want to achieve a particular goal immediately, they aren't afraid of nipping any terrible (and limiting) habits in the bud immediately. This is because they understand the importance of habit formation and how simple habits can change the overall trajectory of their lives.

4. <u>Self-Motivation Lets You Perform Optimally in a Work Environment</u>

To be at your A-game at work, you must understand yourself - your strengths, weaknesses, and everything that makes you unique. When you have identified these, personal motivation allows you to create a profitable pathway to play to your strengths and run away from your weaknesses.

By continuously functioning in your areas of strength, you make better work choices, and you are perceived to be more productive when compared to others. This is why the person who is constantly self-motivated at work performs best and is usually shortlisted for mega opportunities before anyone else.

How to Start Transitioning into Being a Self-Motivated Sigma Male

Now that we have discussed what self-motivation is and how it affects your entire life, it is important that we lay the blocks for understanding exactly how to start transitioning into becoming a self-motivated sigma male.

Do you want to transform from the person always waiting for people to chaperone you to pursue your goals into becoming the person who identifies a thing he wants and goes for it with his whole heart? Here are some steps you must follow.

1. **Take Some Time to Look Within**

One of the major reasons why many people have to deal with a lack of self-motivation is that they are pursuing career paths and investing quality time in ventures they have zero passion for. If you are walking down a difficult road, you don't think of it as exciting; in fact, it is only natural that you would give up or need rescuing every other day.

The first step to becoming self-motivated is to introspect. Find out that thing that makes you motivated and channel your energy towards it. In further sections of this book, we will explore the concept of passion and purpose and help you get started on the right path toward identifying and exploiting yours.

2. **Begin with External Motivation**

Sometimes, internal motivation will not come if you aren't motivated from the outside. If you are acquainted with biology, you must have heard about homeostasis and how it is the body's natural way of adjusting itself to match the stimuli it is getting from the external world. In other words, the body is "motivated" to respond in a specific way to the environment.

In the same way, you may have to rely on some form of external motivation to be internally motivated sometimes. If this is the case with you, do not be afraid to pursue that path and seek external motivation every once in a while.

3. Remember What Made You Start in the First Place

Let's say you are working on a project, and somewhere along the line, you begin to lose the zeal to work on that project. One of the first ways to reboot your self-motivation is by going back to your drawing table and reminding yourself of why you set out on that project in the first place.

Sometimes, all the motivation you need would just be to remind yourself that if you do not make that money from your business, the loan sharks will reclaim your house since you used it as collateral.

4. Maximize Goal Setting

We wouldn't spend much time on the subject of goal setting for now because there's an entire section of this book dedicated to helping you set SMART goals. However, if there's nothing for you to work towards, there'd be absolutely no drive to make things work. This is one of the major reasons why many men are stuck in the loop of being unable to achieve anything worthwhile with their lives. They do not have goals that propel them towards striving to achieve more.

Self-Discipline

Let's make something clear from the start. There is a clear difference between self-motivation and self-discipline. While both of them look like the same thing (when looked at superficially), they are completely different.

Self-discipline is a person's ability to make themselves do the work they have to do, whether they feel like it or not. Self-discipline is what ensures that regardless of the obvious challenges that life tosses at you, you are able to stay the course and see things through until the end. Without self-discipline, it would be difficult to complete projects once you start them out.

Simply put, self-discipline is the power to manage your thoughts, emotions, and behavior when life presents you with a tempting offer to derail you from the achievement of your goals.

The major difference between self-motivation and self-discipline is that while you need self-motivation to get started on projects, you need the self-discipline to stay through until the end. In summary, to have an extraordinary life as a sigma male, you need a delicate blend of self-motivation, to get out of your comfort zone and get started on the actualization of your set goals every day, and self-discipline, to keep your foot on the gas, even when all forms of motivation are out, to complete everything you start.

With these in perspective, here's how you can get started on your journey to developing self-discipline.

How to Develop Self-Discipline

1. Apply All the Tips for Building Self-Motivation

Although they are different, the journey to building self-discipline and self-confidence are intertwined. To get to the place where you can effectively say that you are self-disciplined, you must have developed strong self-motivation. Hence, you have a primary responsibility to internalize all the steps we discussed in the last section of this book and swing into action already.

When you have done that, you are ready for the next stages of developing self-discipline.

2. Identify Your Weaknesses

While self-motivation plays to your strengths (identifying the things you are good at and sticking to them), self-discipline relies heavily on fishing out the things you are terrible at and working on them until the previous lapses aren't evident again.

The first step to becoming a sigma male who is never short on self-discipline is to figure out the parts of your life where you need help. If yours is that you have a habit of eating late and that you never eat healthily, that is a great place to note down and start brainstorming how you can create an effective strategy to get yourself out of that mess you have now identified.

3. Create a Feasible Action Plan

The problem with goals sometimes is that they are overrated. It isn't strange to meet a man who has a lofty idea of what his life will look like in a few years or decades. He has all these ideas that he would be leading a global business with thousands of employees under his care. However, if you take a closer look, you may discover that he has no action plan to move from just having ridiculous goals on paper to living in the reality of what he has written down.

Without a detailed breakdown of how you intend to get to a particular desired aim, you may end up running in circles forever. If your intention is to say a final goodbye to indiscipline, you need an action plan for all your goals.

Take a quick look at what you want to achieve. How do you think you would be able to achieve that goal within the timeframe you have mapped out? What are the steps you must take to get you from point A (where you are currently at the moment) to point B (where you want to be in __ amount of time)?

Those are the steps you clearly want to outline in your action plan.

Here's a demo, 6-step action plan for a new employee who intends to be promoted to becoming a senior staff within the next 5 years.

(Note: this may not be an ideal scenario, but it should be enough to get you started on creating your action plan immediately).

Demo Action Plan

Overall goal: Get promoted to senior staff within the next 8 years (by December 2030)

S/n	Action	Timeline for Execution
1	Learn the ropes of my new position as a new employee and get acquainted with my colleagues	1 Month
2	Get down to work and execute my job description with precision.	2 Months - 1½ years
3.	Discover the decision-makers of the organization and become visible to them (get in their faces, in the right way)	1½ years - 2 years

4	Study other senior managers in the firm and discover the exact qualifications needed for the position I want to fill up. Then, get in their faces and make them like me.	2 years - 2½ years
5.	Get extra qualifications (like a master's degree or even a Ph.D. in a relevant field)	2½ years to 6½ years
6	Pull off a major milestone in the company (something life-changing, like playing a pivotal role in clinching a life-changing client for the organization).	6½ - 7 years
7	Deploying other positioning tactics for maximum visibility and preference over my colleagues	7 - 8 years

While this may not be an ideal situation, sitting down to create this action already puts the bearer in an advantageous position when compared to other employees who have one strategy; to wing it and hope that they will eventually get promoted one day. With this action plan in place, the bearer already knows that he should be focused on achieving these within the next few months.

- Getting to understand the job description as a new employee. Coming to terms with company expectations and getting used to the new work environment.
- Getting into his colleagues' good books so that he can get acquainted with the bureaucracies associated with the corporate workspace.
- Getting closer to the head of his department and (maybe) even asking to be mentored by the person. (The idea behind this is that when the person is promoted, he can also be promoted to fit into his boss' new shoes - as a senior staff of the organization).
- Creating a track record of stellar delivery of assigned tasks and commitment to the organization's core values. This way, there wouldn't be any controversies when the time to be promoted comes.
- Getting any extra academic qualifications needed as prerequisites to the new position he is looking to fill.

With these in place, he knows the exact steps he must take, and coupled with self-motivation, he would be well on his way to becoming a senior staff in the organization within the stipulated time. Do you now see how having a clear action plan for your life and major goals automatically places you at an advantage above everyone else in your corner?

4. Embrace the Truth Early Enough; Life Will Get Boring

The thing is, once you make a commitment to be the guy who takes self-discipline seriously, you'll get to a point where you discover that your life is becoming pretty much boring. This may be because you no longer have as much time on your hands as you used to (because your days are now full of productive and useful activities) or because old friends (who were mostly interested in helping you idly spend your time) have taken the exit door.

In any case, your life is bound to become somehow boring and super predictable once you commit to self-discipline. You'll most likely start living by a to-do list, and this automatically kicks spontaneity out of the door for a long time.

However, don't feel bad. Remind yourself of what you intend to achieve by living the kind of life you are now living.

5. Get an Accountability Partner

We already talked about self-motivation and all the benefits that come with it, right? However, the truth is that there are times that all the self-motivation in the world won't help you. Sometimes, you need someone else to keep you accountable if you would achieve specific things.

Accountability partners are a powerful way of completely embracing self-discipline. When you remember that there's someone out there who would ask you what you have been up to as regards the accomplishment of your goals, you will be inspired to wake up every day and keep acting on the things that matter to you.

6. <u>Go Easy on Yourself</u>

The idea here isn't to make you isolate this point and hold it as your get-out-of-a-tough-day card. The idea here is to remind you that regardless of how hard you try, you will fall short and encounter challenges at some points. It is up to you to take deep breaths, pull back, and strategize when you meet roadblocks.

Emotional Intelligence

This is another important aspect of the life of a successful sigma male that you must come to terms with. This is because humans are mostly emotional (including yourself). No matter how you try to defend it, you may not be able to achieve a lot with your life if you do not understand emotions, how they shape the human being, how they affect your daily decisions, and how to manage your emotions/the emotions of other people.

You may get away with zero emotional intelligence in the beginning. However, a lack of this will lead to unavoidable calamity as you keep growing and fitting bigger roles in your workplace, home, place of worship (if you have any), or even in your family.

What is Emotional Intelligence?

Harvard Health Publishing defines Emotional Intelligence as a measure of your ability to identify and regulate your emotions, identify the emotions of other people and feel/express empathy towards them, and enhance communication/strong interpersonal connections with people using this body of skills known as Emotional Intelligence.

In the corporate world, Emotional Intelligence is known as one of the foundational intelligence quotients every successful human must possess. This is because in the absence of emotional intelligence,

1. **You Would Be an Emotional Wreck**

If you aren't able to keep tabs on your own emotions, you wouldn't know what's happening to you and how to make sure that you stay productive. Without emotional intelligence, Self-motivation is impossible.

2. **You Would Be a Terror to the People Around You**

The way you feel emotions is the same way the people around you feel stuff. If you don't have a clear grip on your emotions, you wouldn't be able to manage yourself when someone behaves in an off-putting way. You never know. It could be because of an internal battle they are going through.

3. You'll End Up Projecting

When you can't identify and deal with your emotions by yourself, there's every tendency that you would end up projecting o the people around you. Have you ever heard about "transferring aggression?" This is usually the result of not being skillful with emotional intelligence.

To lead anything of repute (including a life worthy of emulation), you must be skilled with emotional intelligence. As a social being, you would interact with people regularly (regardless of how hard you work to reduce these interactions), and the earlier you understand and become a master of your emotions (and, by extension, the emotions of others), the better it would be for everyone.

At the foundation of emotional intelligence is the concept of human temperaments and how they affect an everyday man. As a sigma male, it is important that you understand your temperament so that you can finally know why you act the way you do and also create a self-management plan for your temperament's weaknesses while maximizing your temperament's strengths.

You and Your Temperament - Why You Act the Way You Do

At some point in your life, you may have heard someone being described as being choleric or sanguine. You may have also watched people and marveled at how identical twins can be completely different when you take some time to evaluate how they behave and interact with the world at large. The major difference between person A and B and the reason why you may have two or more people who are spitting images of themselves physically but are completely different in character is their temperaments.

If you have paid any attention to this before, you may have heard of the principle of the 4 temperaments. In case you haven't, here's a brief rundown of that principle and what it stands for.

It was around 460-370 BC that Galem took the feedback from previous studies into human behavior and made a medical theory out of them. After extensive research and behavioral analysis, he suggested that every human on the surface of the earth behaved in a certain way because of the constituents of our bodies. According to him, the presence or lack of specific fluids in the body system results in a person being easily irritable, joyful, angry, or even overly withdrawn from life and the world around them.

His studies revealed that there are majorly 4 bodily fluids that are responsible for all these: blood, yellow bile, black bile, and phlegm. As submitted in his studies, people who had an abundance of blood tend to be boisterous, energetic, and warm. Those who, on the other hand, have an abundance of phlegm are intricately withdrawn from life, have an issue responding to situations immediately, and can be easily interpreted as being lazy and lackadaisical. While this theory was mostly combated, it has formed the basis for what is generally accepted as the theory of temperaments in the 21st century, as postulated in a best-selling title, "Why You Act the Way You Do."

In summary, your temperament is a measure of how you behave and interact with the world around you, usually based on biological factors, personal experiences, and other factors that may be beyond the conscious control of the individual. Usually, your temperament remains the same throughout the course of your life. While you may be on the verge of disputing this, it is important to note that most people remain unable to completely change their temperaments. If you know someone who seems to have transformed their temperaments, it is usually because they mastered the act of self-discipline to cover up for the lapses associated with their temperaments while gearing up to take on the responsibilities that life throws at them.

One of the major reasons why it is important that you know and understand your temperaments as a sigma male is because the knowledge you would get from this would play a pivotal role in setting you up for a successful life. When you are exposed to yourself, and you now know the things that trigger you, you are equipped with the information needed to cover up the lapses associated with your temperament and still move on to live a fulfilled life regardless.

Cardinal Temperament Types

With those said, here are the 4 cardinal temperaments types and how each of them affects the quality of a man's life.

1. Choleric

Have you ever desired to be left in the peace and quiet of the corner where you are seated with a drink in hand, only to hear the rambunctious noise of that annoyingly-extroverted friend who announces his arrival by loud laughter and animated chatter with just anyone he meets? If yes, you are most likely dealing with a choleric.

On a scale of 1 to 10, you would rate a choleric a whole 10 when it comes to their socializing skills. One of the first things you would notice about the choleric is an innate ability to be the life of the party, regardless of where he is found and who he has to interact with.

In addition to being the 'salt of the earth,' cholerics have a penchant for being competent leaders, and this is because they have the ability to see "the big picture" and galvanize available resources toward the actualization of the visions they have seen in their mind's eyes. This is why teams with choleric leaders tend to be more productive, action-oriented, and goal-focused when opposed to teams led by people with other dominant temperaments.

They are associated with the element - fire. This means that the choleric is on the lookout for their next biggest result and has little or no patience when things do not go according to their plan.

Here are the things you need to know about the choleric.

Typical Characteristics of a Choleric

Here are some of the typical characteristics associated with cholerics

- **They ooze self-confidence:** It is easy to associate their outgoing spirit with self-confidence, and this is what makes them visible and easy to be spotted in any group.
- **They are super opinionated:** Whatever a choleric feels about a certain idea is what he says. Then again, the choleric man may not have a brain-to-mouth filter, and while this may be irritating to every other person, it makes the choleric man an invaluable member of every group as he can give his unbiased opinion on the group initiatives and tasks.
- **They can come off as domineering:** In a bid to speak their mind (coupled with the fact that choleric men always want to be heard and respected), it is easy to misinterpret them as being controlling.
- **The choleric man is stubborn:** When he believes a thing and voices it out, it may take a supernatural experience to get him to change his mind. When placed in a position of leadership, cholerics can be seen as stubborn and die-hard people.

- **The choleric loves to dream big dreams:** When you engage the choleric in a mentally-stimulating conversation and ask him his goals for the next 5-20 years, you are likely to hear things that would make your jaws fall open in surprise. The choleric takes "dream big" to a whole new level.

Strengths of the Choleric Man

With these traits out in the open, here are some of the typical strengths of the choleric man.

- Considering their ability to be visible in every group, it isn't abnormal to see the choleric occupying some kind of leadership position. In social circles, they are the leaders of the pack.
- The choleric doesn't have issues with associating with people. Hence, he's easily interpreted as kind and lovable. Then again, the choleric would most likely have a million and one friends in every direction he turns.
- The choleric delights in change. Things start feeling boring when they have fallen into a predictable sequence. Hence, it wouldn't be abnormal to see your choleric boss switching things up at work every once in a while (common tasks like reshuffling staff, opening up new branches, and just setting bigger goals would be exciting to him).
- The choleric man doesn't get discouraged easily. Present him with the common test, and how would most likely tell you

that "the glass is half-full." This is because he would rather focus on the good side of everything.

- He sniffs out traitors immediately and corrects group wrongs without fear or favor. This is one of the strengths that make the choleric man a capable leader over any kind of people.
- The choleric man is blessed with an unflinching passion. When he gets an idea up his head, he commits his time and every other resource to make sure it works. Then again, glorying in the after-buzz of achieved goals is one thing a choleric man loves (maybe as much as he loves being famous).

Weaknesses of the Choleric Man

In the face of these strengths, here are some weaknesses you would find as you interact with the choleric.

- A compulsive desire to be in control makes him come off as mean, bossy, and insufferable.
- The choleric is mostly unemotional as he is a rational and logical thinker. He would rather squash down his emotions than admit that he is wrong. This makes the choleric man one of the hardest people to get an "I am sorry" out of. Hence, if you are dealing with a choleric man (maybe as a boss, brother, father, or significant other), you may want to consider forgiving him in advance, even without hearing him apologize (because you may not hear that for a long time).

- In a bid to be in control of every unit of the overall organization, it wouldn't be out of place to see a choleric boss trying to micromanage and losing many things (time, money, clients, productivity, and even company profits) at the same time.
- The choleric has zero-tolerance for mistakes. This makes it difficult for him to put up with newbies in any field (especially in a field that he is emotionally invested in, like his organization or business). If you are this man, you may find yourself being tossed into that never-ending loop of firing staff and having to look for replacement employees over small mistakes that some correction + orientation would have solved.
- To have his way, the choleric man can easily slip into dirty and manipulative ways. This is one of the major challenges the choleric man may face, especially if he intends to get into public offices (like becoming a politician of any kind).

Self-Management Strategies for Choleric Men

If you are a choleric man and you saw yourself in the words of this last section of the book, there's no need to bury your head in shame and wish for a rebirth. You are a good man, and even if you may end up making a number of mistakes (and bad choices) in your lifetime due to your temperament, here are some effective self-management tactics you can use to cover up for identified behavioral lapses.

- Ensure your team is made up of people with diverse temperaments. There has to be someone at the helm of activities in your organization (alongside yourself) who is permitted to be the Yin to your Yang and who can smack you on the head when you want to make wonky decisions.

   This way, you can have the advantages that come with your temperament while still holding on to the blessings associated with having an eagle-eye view of every situation.
- Create a system that allows you to carefully evaluate every step before taking them. Considering that the choleric man is bent on having his way almost every time, one of the things he may not be able to effectively do is think things through. To avoid running into challenges every other time, make sure you critically look before you leap.
- Ensure you have a sanguine as part of your managerial board. Sanguines tend to effectively balance cholerics out. You will discover why as you keep reading this chapter.

2. <u>Sanguine</u>

The sanguine is mostly characterized by his tendency to be boisterous and all over the place. His loudness introduces him every time he walks into a room, and he can quickly become the life of the party because he has a penchant for telling huge (and mostly embellished) tales.

One of the things you would easily notice when you work with a sanguine is that it is almost next to impossible to get him to relax long enough to finish any seemingly complicated task. Just like the choleric, he is always in a state of motion and does well in public spaces.

Strengths of the Sanguine Man

Here are some things that make the sanguine man likable:

- **He is mostly a social butterfly:** Because of his ability to be the life of the party every time, the sanguine is mostly loved by the people he meets. Then again, his storytelling skills are on another level, and this inherent ability to entertain makes people easily flock toward him.
- **He is a powerful orator and an excellent communicator:** These attributes make him the perfect face when you seek stellar PR for your organization. Do you need someone that can speak to a mob of people, wow their socks off, and convince them to take a specific action? Your sanguine guy is the best person for this.
- **The sanguine tends to be in touch with the emotions of others:** When the sanguine laughs, he does that from the depths of his heart, and he genuinely wants to see the people in his world happy and satisfied as well. The sanguine is one of the best people to have as a close find because he knows exactly when the mood of the person next to him shifts and

would do all he can to lift their spirits back up when they feel like they are about to falter.

- **"Forgive and forget" was written with their name on it:** The sanguine believes in living in the present. Hence, he has little or no business holding on to past hurts. He is mostly the kind of person that would forgive you in advance, even when you haven't apologized to him.
- **He has healthy self-esteem:** The sanguine walks around with an air of importance because he knows he is important. He doesn't seek external validation, and this is one factor that can make him stand out from an entire mob of people at work if he is able to keep still for long enough and concentrate on doing the work he has to do.

Weaknesses of the Sanguine Man

- **His self-confidence can easily be interpreted as arrogance or cockiness:** This is one of the first challenges the sanguine man would face in a corporate setting. Because he knows he is all the validation he needs, he hardly defers to people. Those who do not understand him would think of him as being arrogant. Guess who wouldn't take this well at all? The choleric!
- **The sanguine is prone to telling lies:** Because of his penchant for telling juicy stories that are mostly embellished, the sanguine man may find himself on the verge of telling

little white lies every time he is in a conversation. If this goes undetected and unmanaged, he might make a habit of lying, and people may begin to notice it.

When others start noticing it, they may have trust issues with him, and this can affect the entire quality of the sanguine's life and relationships.

- **His attention-seeking disposition can affect his entire life:** The sanguine loves to be at the center of attention everywhere he is found. While this can be a competitive edge for him (in terms of career growth opportunities), it comes with the downside of making him feel inferior when the people around him do not seem to pay him any heed. This can sometimes make it difficult for the sanguine to have and maintain strong relationships over time because once he discovers that he is no longer at the center of that person's attention, he zooms off to the next conquest - no matter how this change affects his life.
- **Impulsive:** Whenever you see a sanguine man, you are likely to find him seeking out his next adventure. While it is great to seek fun and take risks in life, the sanguine, just like a choleric, has the tendency of jumping at anything before he even asks himself what he is doing.

In addition, his impulsive nature, if not corrected ad kept in check, can make him an organizational wreck when he is placed in specific positions in a company., for example, when a sanguine is in charge of the finances of a multinational company...

- **They wear their hearts on their sleeves:** The sanguine is expressive and not afraid to show what he feels. He cries, laughs, and plays with the people around him. On the downside, people can easily take advantage of his empathy and generosity to rip him off.

Self-Management Strategies for Sanguine Men

Here are some thig the sanguine can do to keep his temperament from being his undoing.

- The sanguine male should do well to remind himself on a regular basis that he shouldn't always be the one speaking. It is okay to stand back and allow other people to talk as well. After all, what's a conversation if he's the one doing most of the talking?

  In addition to making him become even more endearing to people, it reduces the chances that he would run into the challenge associated with talking a lot, that challenge of blowing things out of proportion and exaggerating at every given opportunity. This simple lifestyle change can positively affect the life of the sanguine for a long time to come.

- The sanguine man's boisterous nature doesn't only stop at social gatherings. His tendency to jump at almost everything that comes his way usually leads him to develop unhealthy eating habits. Because he eats almost anything and has a robust appetite, it isn't unusual to see the sanguine man with a lot more weight than he can manage. This tendency also affects the quality of his life if he doesn't take specific steps to mitigate it.

The first step a sanguine man should take to eliminate the risk of becoming obese (especially if being overweight runs in his family) is to take out some time to consult with a nutritionist. During this time, he is to obtain a meal plan that he should strongly follow up with.

If done well and followed, this should reduce his chances of getting overweight and being bogged down with all the challenges that accompany being overweight.

- The sanguine man's biggest advantage would be to get himself an accountability partner. His boisterous nature makes him a great beginner but never a great finisher. To ensure that he always stays on track and completes everything his hands start, the sanguine man could use an accountability partner.

This would even be better if this accountability partner is someone superior to him, who has what it takes to discipline him when he begins to veer off from set goals.

- As a sanguine man who needs a lot of assurance and attention from people, you would benefit from the simple lifestyle change of using affirmations. Instead of waiting for people (who may never remember to appreciate you) to do that and getting depressed when they don't, why not take that responsibility into your own hands and spend time appreciating yourself for how awesome you are?

3. Melancholic

The dictionary defines this temperament as a state of being irascible or depressed, usually associated with the abundance of black bile in a person's body system. The melancholic man is usually characterized by his lonesomeness and preference for being all by himself. His reflective mood makes him come off as 'depressed.'

If you walk into a room with just a sanguine and melancholic who do not know themselves, you will probably recognize the melancholic by simply looking at how he would be seated down with a hunch in his back, like he doesn't want to have anything to do with the world.

In social gatherings, the melancholic man is usually the last person to stand up and meet new people. He would rather stand back and allow people to come to him, even as he assesses them with keen eyes while they walk up to him.

Strengths of the melancholic man

- **They tend to be good with theatre and arts:** This is usually a result of the bottled-up emotions they feel. Anytime they have to express their creativity through acting, singing, painting, and fashion, they let go. Then again, if they have to do something they are truly passionate about, they usually produce stellar work.

  All these are due to the fact that the melancholic man is mostly reflective, observant, and creative. Although he doesn't say a lot, he sees everything and has a million thoughts rolling through his mind at every second. Art gives him the platform to express himself without any fear of being judged.

- **Independence:** One of the most independent temperament types you would ever meet in your lifetime are melancholics. Since they love spending their time by themselves and do not seek a lot of social interactions, they are mostly left to learn how to fend for themselves early enough.

  The melancholic man believes that his own validation is the best thing that has happened to him. Then again, he doesn't seek a lot of communication with others. The melancholic man won't mind spending an entire week indoors if he has everything he needs to make the most of his week.

- **His creativity makes him stand out at work:** His ability to look at complicated projects, make sense of them, and draft effective strategies to get out of every mess serves him properly at work. When he gets out of his head and into the work he has to do, the melancholic man is unstoppable and a great asset to his entire organization.
- **The melancholic man is orderly:** You may never find one thing out of place in his space. His reflective nature makes him take notice of things that are out of shape immediately, and he does something to fix them all as soon as possible. Then again, this attribute helps him to maintain strong relationships with the people that matter to him.
- **He would be the best fit for any creative work:** Arts, writing, coding, and tech jobs that require intense attention to detail, name them. The melancholic man's calmness makes him the perfect fit for all these types of roles. Give him anything that requires him to think deeply over a subject and provide solutions to seemingly complex issues, and he would excel effortlessly.

Weaknesses of the melancholic man

- **His moods change easily:** Considering the thoughts that fly through his mind with the speed of light, it isn't uncommon to find out that the melancholic man's mood changes in dramatic ways. One second, he is beaming and happy. The next second, he withdraws into his shell and wants to shut the entire world away.

- **He isn't the easiest person to befriend:** His mood swings, coupled with his tendency to look detached from life and even hostile (when he sits with a glare on his face), make the melancholic man one of the most challenging people to befriend. He ends up being one of the most loyal people you would eventually meet in your life, but the challenge is to get past the initial walls he would put up.
- **The melancholic man lives mostly in his head:** Every time he is about to start something new (or take any risk at all), the voices in his head intensify and would most likely keep him from at least trying. The melancholic man fights with perfectionism every day and can sometimes be a pessimist.

Before embarking upon any new project, his mind analyzes things ad shows him a million and one ways everything can go south. This makes it almost impossible for the melancholic man to start anything all by himself. He is an excellent finisher but a terrible starter.

- **Always worried:** The melancholic man is characterized by having a strong emotional component in life. He tends to spend the best parts of his days worrying and stressing about the things that are beyond his control.

This worry affects his productivity and mostly makes him feel like he is at the same spot year after year. These feelings further contribute to his depression, and the vicious cycle continues.

- **Cynical:** The worst way to get a melancholic man to hate you is by criticizing or making jest of him. He finds it hard to come to terms with the fact that people can just tease themselves and mean no harm while at it. For him, every word is to be taken to heart and deconstructed accordingly so as to ascertain what was going on in the mind of the speaker at the point of making such a comment.

This makes the melancholic man a cynical person to be around. The melancholic will throw a fit if as much as 1 single criticism is thrown his way. This can affect his entire day and make him feel as though he is worthless to the person criticizing him - even if the person meant it for good.

Self-management strategies for melancholic men

- You would benefit a lot as a follower or employee, not just as a vision bearer. This is because the grit needed to start and grow a business may not be inherent in you at first. However, if you insist that you want to start and grow your own business, remember that self-mastery skills are there to help you cover up for these lapses.

- If you have a melancholic man on the leadership team of any organization, ensure you have a choleric leader as well because both of them would do well to balance each other out.
- The choleric leader sees the big picture, sets the audacious goals, and motivates everyone to move in the direction of the greatest good. The melancholic leader sees the smaller details, defines the opportunity cost of moving in a specific direction, draws up the implementation plan, and keeps everyone accountable for the progress they seek.
- The melancholic man can do well by taking extra courses and programs that seek to build up his confidence and self-esteem. This is because he may keep losing opportunities if he doesn't master the art of walking up to strangers, introducing himself, and starting profitable conversations with them.
- If you are a melancholic man, constantly remind yourself to strap a smile on your face every single time you go out for a public function. You look more approachable when people do not see you scowling.
- Stay within areas of interest. If you don't feel like becoming a doctor, lawyer, or public figure, do well to steer clear of those career paths.

4. Phlegmatic

This is the last temperament type we would be paying attention to. The phlegmatic man is known for being slow to everything (even worse than the melancholic). He looks uninspired, acts uninspired, and is most averse to confrontations or challenges of any kind.

The phlegmatic sees life as either black or white. He doesn't seem to be able to wrap his head around the fact that he needs to step out of his comfort zone and make things work if he wants anything good out of his life. He believes that if it is meant for him, it will find its way to him. This is one of the dangerous beliefs that keeps him mostly in the backseat of life because everyone else goes to grab what they want, while he sits at the back wishing for what he should have gone out to grab.

The easiest way to spot a phlegmatic man is to check out the slowest member of every group. Who is the last to respond to simple instructions? Who detests the idea of a face-off, even if it is about standing up for something he knows is his right? He is most likely going to be the phlegmatic man.

Strengths of the Phlegmatic Man

- **He is a peacemaker:** One of the major strengths of the phlegmatic man is that he is addicted to peace. Do you need someone who can mediate almost any fight (regardless of how bad things are) and make all parties lay down their knives almost immediately? Your phlegmatic man is your best bet.

Then again, the phlegmatic man, because of this, is one of the easiest men to live and interact with. He is super agreeable and wouldn't give you much opposition on anything at all. This can easily prove to be a challenge down the line.

- **He is a powerful negotiator:** Rather than do anything that would keep him uncomfortable, the phlegmatic man would figure out the most diplomatic way to talk himself and every other person out of it. This is a great attribute because it makes him able to win arguments and convince people to move in any direction he wants when it is favorable for him.

  The only challenge is that the phlegmatic man hardly draws on this superpower when the chips are down. He only uses it as a last resort.

- **Consistency:** The phlegmatic man is one of the most consistent people you would meet in any given situation. He is considerate, balanced, takes his time to make decisions, and understands the place of time in almost everything. On this front, he always makes a good boss.

- **Friends:** Because of his agreeable nature, the phlegmatic man makes a good friend if you are looking for someone who would be consistent with you. He isn't afraid to commit in this regard and would probably be in your life after many years, all things equal.

He may not be the most outgoing man in the group, but he is the one that would give you a listening ear when you desperately need one, help you through any situation you may have found yourself in without throwing stones, and he is the least judgmental person you would meet.

Weaknesses of the Phlegmatic Man

- **He can be stubborn:** The worst part about his stubbornness is that it is tinged with a mix of quietness. Hence, when he places his feet on the brakes and decides that he doesn't want to do something, you may even find it difficult to know that he is the reason why you aren't hitting your goals.

  On a corporate level, the phlegmatic can easily hide behind a ton of other people and influence the quality of their output from where he is. When he isn't functioning as a one-man team or leading something, it is difficult to gauge his output if you don't pay close attention.

  As far as the choleric is concerned, the phlegmatic is his biggest nightmare because the phlegmatic is the only temperament he may not be able to control.

- **He can easily lose himself while trying to please others**: Since the phlegmatic man is the worst enemy of face-offs, he does all he can to please everyone around him. While this is great, it can be an impediment to his own growth because he doesn't know how to say 'no,' even when things don't work out well for him.

- **He is arguably the most uninspired person you would ever have on any team:** The phlegmatic man doesn't understand why he should stretch himself over anything. A part of him knows that he should be pursuing his goals, but he never seems to get it into his head that people just don't become successful without doing any kind of work.

  So, he would give up whenever he had to do any kind of work. Although he is a creative person, he prioritizes his comfort over anything else. Then again, his lackadaisical attitude towards life can make him lose many opportunities that he should have snagged.

Self-Management Tips for a Phlegmatic Man

- Surround yourself with cholerics and melancholics. Let there be other people that can motivate and encourage you to commit toward the achievement of all your set goals.
- The biggest need of every phlegmatic man is an implementation plan. He doesn't need to be scolded when he falls short of expectations. He just needs a step-by-step breakdown of what he must do, how he must do it, and the steps that ensure he will do the needful when the time comes.
- Accountability will be the goldmine in the life of every phlegmatic. No matter how self-motivated he believes he is, a

time will come when his dominant temperament swoops in, and he will just need those external eyes to keep himself going or risk falling back to how he used to be a while ago.

In this section, we have broken down the 4 major temperaments there are. The aim of doing this is to help you locate yourself in the quadrant so that you can better understand who you are and how to manage your temperaments.

Take the self-management principles seriously, as they would help you maximize your potential as a sigma male, regardless of your dominant temperament. It is also important to note that everyone is a mixture of two or more of these temperaments.

Your dominant temperament is the primary temperament (the one you manifest by default). The secondary temperament comes up occasionally and as the needs arise. Bear this in mind while you try to find yourself on the quotient, as you may see yourself showcasing the characteristics of more than one temperament type.

Goal Setting, Goal Pursuit, and Goal Actualization

One of the Sigma male's superpowers (the skills that keep him at peak performance) is his uncanny ability, to be honest with himself and set goals that keep him on his feet. The everyday man, on the other hand, has an inkling of what he wants to achieve in most aspects of his life, appreciates the work he has to do to get to where he wants to be, but never sees the need to grab a seat, get a pen and paper, and set strategic goals that would lead him to where he desires to get.

As far as he is concerned, what's the need to set goals since he always ends up getting stuff done anyways?

What he doesn't know is that if he is able to achieve any sort of thing in his life, he would be able to achieve a lot more if only he could take a while to master the art of goal setting, goal pursuit, and goal actualization.

The sigma male, on the other hand, knows these principles and abides by them. So, if you would want to become that sigma male who lives at the zenith of his abilities and has the whole world at his feet, pay attention as we take you through these concepts ad show you how to apply them to your life immediately.

Goal Setting

If you are living and active in today's world, it is safe to assume that you must have heard this word used in some way before now. It could be at an event or a workshop, or you may have even seen it while scrolling through your Instagram feed.

The thing is chances that goal setting is an entirely new phenomenon to you are quite slim. In fact, even if you believe that you have never set a goal in life, you might be surprised to know that you have set and actualized so many goals in your lifetime (regardless of how young you are). Maybe it was to talk to your crush in high school before the end of a specific term or to shed a particular amount of weight before 2 months elapsed. Chances that you have set and smashed some goals in your lifetime are plenty.

However, if you have consciously committed yourself to setting and achieving goals, you can attest to how organized your life typically becomes almost instantly. Simply because you give yourself something to look forward to every single day, you eliminate your chances of moving as the day leads you, but you give yourself a laid-down pathway to follow so that you can maximize every single day.

In this section of the book, let us take a quick look at what goal setting entails.

According to Wikipedia, "goal setting involves the development of an action plan designed specifically to motivate and guide a person or group toward the actualization of a goal." A goal, in this context, is the desired outcome or predefined end that someone would want to achieve after a period of time.

Simply put, goal setting is the art of taking a peek into the future (to define what you would want to achieve after a period of time) and mapping out effective strategies that would take you from where you are right now to the place you desire to be. When compared to wishful thinking, goal setting is more elaborate because it ties time to the achievement of every goal and also brings the individual steps that would be taken to achieve that goal into consideration.

Goal setting is mostly about planning, strategy, and personal domination.

Now that we have critically analyzed the concept of goal setting, one of the next questions that would come to mind is why it is important for anyone to set goals. If you can still get stuff done anyways, why should you go through the stress of setting goals and keeping yourself accountable for the process of achieving them?

Well, here are some reasons why goal setting is non-negotiable for you as a sigma male.

1. Goal setting is the key to an enviable future. The man who has become a mast at the art of setting and smashing goals is the one who has complete control over the trajectory of his life. Everything you would achieve as a sigma male is tied to your ability to set and smash your goals. This ranges from your emotional life and relationships to the success of your career and even to your physical and mental health.

   Goal setting is the building block of every successful life you admire today.

2. Goal setting helps you to overcome procrastination, roll up your sleeves, and get down to the unexciting part of doing every work that must be done to get to where you should be. Without goal setting, you may just be stuck in your head, thinking/fantasizing about the things that could happen for you. However, you may be stuck in a nasty web of

procrastination. With goal setting, you deal with procrastination once and for all and get started on your way to living a life that is characterized by swift and prompt action-taking.

3. Goal setting deals with the "how." When you apply the principles of goal setting that will be discussed shortly, you move from just having lofty visions in your mind toward the actualization of those visions you have had. Also, goal setting permits you to see the actions you must take to achieve a specific target in your life. By this, you are well-equipped to take the necessary steps needed for your growth and evolution as a sigma male.

Elements of Achievable Goals

The concept of SMART goals was first introduced by George Doran, James Cunningham, and Arthur Miller in 1981. Although the model has undergone a lot of modifications over time, it still holds one of the most powerful models for goal setting that has stood the test of time all these decades later.

This goal-setting model teaches that if you would have any kind of success with goal setting and actualization, your goals have to meet the SMART criteria. Let's take a quick look at what the SMART criterium is all about.

- Specific

If you must be successful with your goal-setting exercises, your goals must be Specific. That is, every goal you set must be well-defined, unambiguous, and clear in its expression. The SMART goal setting model teaches that if you set a goal that is not specific, you wouldn't be able to achieve anything because you wouldn't set relevant KPIs, you wouldn't be able to track your progress, and you wouldn't even know the relevant action you must take to achieve those goals in the first place.

An example of a specific goal is "I will lose weight."

- Measurable

This deals with the ability of your overarching goal to be broken down into smaller bits so that you can easily measure if you are moving toward the actualization of your goal or if you are drifting farther away from it. If you are unable to measure your main goals, there would be no yardstick for determining if you are successful or not after an appreciable amount of time has passed.

Refining the example from point 1 above, the goal can become "I will lose 20 pounds…'

- Achievable

While it is important and dignifying to set your sights on the stars, it doesn't make sense if you set goals that your mind doesn't yet consider as achievable. For your goal to be achievable, you must have seen others crushing it. Your mind must first come to relate with the goal, not as something that is beyond reach, but as something that you can grasp with the right kind of work and effective strategies.

- Realistic

This somehow ties back to the last point we already made. For you to achieve any goal, it has to be realistic. Realistic, in this context, means that the goal has to be something you have seen as being achievable by you. Then again, it has to tie back to your life's purpose every time if you would be able to pursue it with everything you have inside you.

Typical example: it doesn't make sense to set a goal that you would earn $5,000,000 in annual revenue in 2023 if all you have ever earned as annual revenue all your life is just $100,000. To make your goal realistic, how about you start with something smaller, like $1,000,000?

No. The idea isn't to belittle yourself. It is simply to give you a springboard that you can leverage to strengthen your confidence and resolve. When you have hit the goal of $1,000,000, it becomes much easier to draft and implement strategies that can take you to $5,000,000 in the following years.

- Timely or Time-Bound

A goal remains a wish until the time is tied to it. If you do not have a timeframe for the actualization of every goal you have set, you won't achieve it (life is honestly that simple). For one, you would have to deal with insane levels of procrastination when there's no time in the equation.

Then again, tying time to the achievement of your goals gives you a sense of urgency. There's no better way to get yourself inspired than to leave the bed and go pursue your dreams every single day if you don't tie time to the achievement of your set goals.

When you add this element to the example we have used so far; a SMART goal can be "I will lose 20 pounds by August 2022."

See? That goal is Specific, Measurable, Realistic (depending on the nuances surrounding the individual), and Timely. Swipe this format the next time you are about to set goals and watch your productivity spike.

How to Effectively Set Goals

It is one thing to know the elements of goals that get actualized. It is another thing to know what you must do if you want to effectively set goals that get accomplished. In any case, here's how to set goals that you can move on to crush.

- **Perform a brainstorming session:** It is impossible to set the right goals if you do not take your brain along with you in these goal-setting sessions. When you switch your brain off and set goals with just your emotions, you'd get frustrated once your emotions have shifted over to something else.

So, start every goal-setting session with a proper brainstorming mini-session. In a few minutes, take a pen and paper and:

- A. Make a list of -7 cardinal things you would love to happen for you right now or within a specific timeframe.
- B. Ensure that this list covers the cardinal aspects of your life. Talk about notable things in areas of your life like your finances, health, relationships, career, etc.

When you are done with this exercise, you are ready to move on to the next one.

- **Prioritize:** As much as you intend to achieve a lot of things with your life, you are only one person who's got just 24 hours in his day. Which of these things will have the greatest impact on the overall quality of your life if it were to happen for you within the stipulated time you have identified?

  When you have identified the most pressing 2 or 3, focus on them and shelve the rest for a much later date.

- **Isolate and tie them back to your life's purpose (at the moment):** When you have isolated the most important 3 from your list, take a minute to think about how they tie back to your life's assignment or your purpose at the moment. How will these goals help you to live a more fulfilled life and positively affect humanity while you are at it?

This question, when answered, can give you all the emotional and mental kick you need to move from just having a goal on paper to getting up every morning intent on doing all it takes to get yourself to achieve the goals you have set.

Even if you do not have a holistic sense of your life's purpose, tie these back to the things that matter to you at the moment.

- **Follow the blueprint we discussed in the last section:** Now that you know what you should be focused on and why it is time to create a goal out of every focus area you have identified. Use the SMART blueprint to turn this vision into an achievable goal.

Interestingly, every vision on your list can be translated into a goal. It would just take some more brainstorming and strategy. However, you should be able to come up with just the right goals when you are done with this exercise.

Goal Pursuit and Actualization

When you are done putting pen to paper and setting your SMART goals, the next question you must ask and answer is how you intend to pursue and actualize the goals you have now set. This is where many people get it wrong.

Many men believe that all they need to do is have a seat, pick up a pen/paper, and write out ridiculous goals that they don't even see as attainable for themselves. They make little or no plans to achieve those goals, and neither do they lay down any strategy to ensure that they are committed to the course.

The sad thing is that life doesn't work this way.

If you intend to crush any goals you have set for yourself, no matter how SMART they are, you have to set up structures that allow you to effectively pursue and actualize those goals. Here are a few structures you can erect in your life right now to ensure that you hit your next set of goals.

- **Making the necessary habit changes:** It is impossible to hit big goals with the tiny habits you have had until now, those habits that kept you from accomplishing all that you said you would in the past. While this isn't the chapter where we would be doing justice to the subject of habits, it is important to note that if you want to live a life of crushed goals after crushed goals, you must look within so that you can spot those habits that are limiting your progress.

    After that, you must commit to changing them immediately.

- **Self-discipline and motivation:** We have already hinted at what these 2 are and how they are vital to the actualization of your life's purpose. To achieve any goal at all, you have to exercise discipline over yourself. You would have to wake up and roll out of bed every morning, no matter how stressed out or uninspired you may feel.

Constantly remind yourself that your feelings have nothing to do with the actualization of your goals.

- **Accountability:** There are some goals that you don't stand the chance of accomplishing if you approach them as a one-man squad. Simply put, accountability is admitting that you may be incapable of meeting specific targets all by yourself and opening yourself up to be answerable to another person.

Sigma males who have understood the power of accountability and tapped into it have been able to crush every goal they have set and literally transform their lives within the shortest possible time.

- **Visualization and Affirmation:** In a subsequent chapter of this book, we will explore the relationship between the sigma male and his spiritual side. Spirituality is a strong component of success, and this is where visualization comes into play.

When you visualize something, you see yourself living in that reality. Then again, where your attention goes is where your energy will flow, and the law of attraction will ensure that you get what you always think and imagine in your mind.

One way to keep yourself on track to achieve your goals is to back every strategic action with visualization and affirmations. Keep thinking and saying it until you manifest it.

- **Review your progress and celebrate yourself:** For every goal that you will eventually achieve, you have to set KPIs as well. Key Performance Indicators (KPIs) are smaller steps that, when accomplished, show that you are on the right track toward the actualization of the goals you have set for yourself.

Let's take the earlier example of losing weight, for example. The overall goal was to lose 20 pounds within a few months. An effective KPI could be to shed 5 pounds every month (30 days). So, if, at the end of the 1st 30 days, he discovers that he wasn't able to shed 5 pounds, he would immediately know that he must change his strategy or review his entire weight loss process to see what is going wrong with him.

Then again, when you record a win, celebrating yourself is imperative. This way, you inspire yourself to keep striving for the ultimate goal you have in mind. Then again, KPIs remind you that the main goal is possible.

Habits - the Building Blocks of Your Success

Have you ever heard this expression being used to describe someone; "They have bad/good habits"? If you have, you have probably gotten the vibe that habits are vital toward the success or failure of any person - especially the sigma male.

Another superpower the sigma male has is that he has mastered himself over time such that he has been able to create powerful habits that lead him to the actualization of his goals and ambitions per time. The first thing you must know about habits is that if you want to live an extraordinary life, your habits must be in sync with your purpose and the goals you have set per time.

You cannot have a goal to become a millionaire by a specific time of the year and still allow your life to be run by the negative habits that left you out in the cold just a few years back; habits like excessive borrowing, zero savings, gambling, and zero plans for investments.

As you can already see, if your life isn't built on solid habits, you may be caught up in a web of wishful thinking while still exerting physical pressure to set the goals that never get accomplished.

So, while working on yourself, it is important that you pay attention to your habits immediately. Some of the things you'd learn in this chapter may sting your ego. However, you must take the necessary action if you intend to get favorable results at the end of the day.

Are you ready to overhaul your habits?

What Are Habits and Why Are They Absolutely Important?

Habits are routine behaviors that we carry out repeatedly and, in most cases, subconsciously. Usually, habits start out like every other thing until you have practiced them long and frequent enough for those actions and thought patterns to be registered in your subconscious mind. Once this happens, your subconscious takes over, and you would find yourself carrying out these actions without even planning to.

The sad thing about habits is that they are effective as they set your life on the path to success or even failure. As easy as it is to acquire good habits (under the right situations), it seems even easier to acquire bad habits.

There are many reasons why habits are vital. Here are some of them.

1. Habits make your life more predictable, less strenuous, and more productive. Research carried out revealed that about 43% of every man's daily activities are performed out of habit. So, from making your bed in the morning to say a prayer, brushing your teeth, and fixing your favorite blend of black coffee, life would be more strenuous if it weren't for the brain's ability to record relevant data and create habit loops out of them.

2. Considering that many of your daily actions are the result of the habits you have formed, it is safe to say that good habits save you time. Instead of having to worry over how many cubes of sugar you should pour into your coffee mug, your brain steps in and allows you to carry that action out on autopilot. This frees up more space in your conscious mind so you can carry out other activities that matter to you.

   You are able to multitask because of these habit loops created by your brain. Imagine the amount of time you can save simply by listening to a podcast while doing your laundry at the same time?

3. Habits play a significant role in mind management. If you have made a habit of dwelling on demoralizing thoughts, you will find yourself being cooped up in that hole of depression, and this would, in turn, affects the overall quality of your life when you find out that you no longer have what it takes to perform at your peak.

How to Identify and Crush Limiting Habits

Now that we have settled the conversation of what habits are and why they are important in your growth journey, the next thing we need to know is how to identify and eliminate bad habits from our lives.

First of all, what is a bad habit?

Simply put, a bad habit is a habit that doesn't give you the desired result you want to see in your life. It is that action that once you take, it feels like you are retrogressing instead of taking strategic steps toward the actualization of your life's assignment and goals as a sigma male.

It is also important to note that many bad habits feel rewarding and satisfying at the moment, but their longer-term results are less than desirable. For example, the man who takes a stick of cigarettes and a bottle of alcohol every day he returns from work (to ease the tension he has dealt with the entire day) will feel relieved and even ecstatic in the moment. However, when time passes and his health begins to take a beating from his bad habits/wrong choices, he may not be able to take back the actions he made all those years ago.

Take this as a rule of thumb. If it feels too good right now, it may not be the best habit for you to imbibe. Before you argue about that, think about the thrill that comes from stuffing your mouth full of junk food and having the sugary tastes explode all over your taste buds. It is great, right?

However, think about the side effects of gorging on junk food for an appreciable amount of time.

With these in perspective, here's how to identify bad habits.

How to Identify Terrible Habits

1. Start by admitting that you have a couple of less-than-the-best habits in your life right now. It is impossible to spot out and eliminate what you haven't yet admitted its existence. When you have done this, keep an open mind and get yourself ready for the next steps.
2. Every bad habit meets the following criteria. If, after careful analysis, you discover that the habit in question meets these criteria, it is a bad one:
   - It breaks societal customs. Hence, the general public tends to frown at it.
   - If you exert your willpower, you stand the chance of stopping the activity for good. This is as opposed to situations like medical conditions that you do not have any control over.
3. Bad habits have a toll on your mental health. Once the initial high that accompanies that action is passed, you may find yourself regretting the action or not looking out for the effects it will have on your mind and body in the long run.

You just know that it is bad. Whenever you indulge yourself in a bad habit, your mind first tells you that you have just indulged yourself in something you shouldn't have. Then again, if someone witnessed that activity, they most likely confirmed your fears.

How to Crush Terrible Habits

Think about it for one second. The reason why you have to go through the stressful process of identifying negative habits is so that you can commit time and energy to get rid of them once and for all. After identifying the habits you want to be rid of, here are the activities you must engage in to get rid of them immediately.

1. **Learn, Don't Act**

This may go against everything you know about bad habits. You may have learned that the best form of defense against bad habits is an offense. While this is true to an extent, the best way to attract and send bad habits packing at first is to understand exactly what that habit is all about.

Learn about the cues. What triggers you to act in a specific way? For example, do you only crave a stick of cigarettes when you are extremely stressed or worried about something? Do you only spend your mornings scrolling away your precious time on Instagram when you had a pretty rough night?

Take the first 2 weeks to consciously study the loop of that particular habit and determine the triggers for the habit. When you have accomplished this, you are set for the next stage of conquering those bad habits for good.

2. Eliminate the Triggers

After identifying the triggers (the situations that kick off the urge to indulge yourself in a specific bad habit), the next action plan would be to consciously eliminate those triggers. It is almost impossible to tackle a bad habit if the triggers are still there.

So, if your trigger is "stress," commit to walking away from situations that rile you up and make you feel like the weight of the world is on your shoulders. To achieve this, sometimes, you may have to consider changing your physical environment, as your physical environment can also be the trigger for your bad habit.

3. Make a Structured Plan to Replace Your Bad Habits

You do not wish your way out of a bad habit, and everything you do without a laid-down plan is simply "wishing." To break out of an identified bad habit, make a plan on what you are going to do once the urge to carry out that specific habit comes up again.

For example, when you feel the urge to pick up a stick cigarette again (because you are stressed after a long day at work), a plan would say to pick up an apple instead.

Note that when creating a plan, you should focus on replacing the identified action (habit) with another action that looks and feels like it but has healthier effects on your body. In this example, eating an apple and smoking a cigarette all involve stuffing something inside your mouth, and this can give the brain the vibes you want it to have. Although the second option is infinitely healthier, you have mostly taken the stress off yourself; the stress of sticking your hands into your pockets and pretending that nothing is happening the next time you are tempted to smoke a cigarette.

4. Make It Difficult

Studies have revealed again and again that humans are obsessed with following the path of least resistance. This is simply the principle that teaches that the mind of a man is constantly in a state of weighing options and automatically opting in for any option that looks like it wouldn't require a lot of mental exertion immediately.

For example, when you are faced with the option of washing a heap of dirty laundry and just curling up on the couch with a cup of sweet tea in one hand and with your favorite Netflix show in the distance, your mind automatically makes a choice without consulting you.

The proof that your subconscious mind made a choice without consulting you lies in the fact that you would be tempted to choose option 2 because it seems more rewarding and doesn't require a lot of mental/physical exertion to make it work.

Take this same principle and apply it to the study of habits. One sure way to stop your bad habits is by making it harder to indulge in them. The more you make it difficult to indulge in them, the easier it would be to stop them altogether.

Take the smoking habit, for example. One way to make it difficult would be to discard all packs of cigarettes in your house. The next time you are tempted to smoke, and you remember that you have to get changed, get into your car, and complete a 10 to 20-minute drive simply because you are in need of a smoke, you will rethink the idea. Swipe this activity for every bad habit you want to change.

5. [Sooner or Later, You'd Be Needing Some Company]

Breaking out of bad habits can be tedious. Sometimes, you would find yourself craving those bad habits so much that you would want to toss all your hard work and discipline aside, only to feel the thrill of that bad habit you have decided to stop.

This is why it is important that you have a partner who can walk with you on this self-recovery journey.

When the urge to indulge yourself becomes unbearable, is there someone you can call out for, and they would run to your aid? If you have one already, congratulations. If not, accountability is an important part of dealing with negative habits once and for all.

6. [Give Yourself Time]

It took you years of consistency to build that habit, regardless of how limiting and negative it is. You don't expect to have at it for a few days and find out that it is all gone with a shining good habit in its place. No, life hardly works that way.

Studies show that you need to carry out an activity consistently, for at least 21 days, before it morphs into a full-blown habit. During this time, you would have so many failures, and you may slip on your resolve a couple of times. Do not let these dampen your resolve to break out of the bad habits.

Every time you fall short, pick yourself up and try again until you accomplish what you seek.

Daily Routines of a True Sigma Male

"Success leaves clues."

If you have studied the lives of successful people, you must have heard this saying. It means that when you pay attention to the life of a successful person, you can find out some of the things they did to become the person you admire right now. In the same vein, if you intend to be a true Sigma Male, you have to study the lives of successful Sigma Males and find out what their daily habits are like.

If you can do this and model these habits for yourself, you are already well on your way to becoming the kind of man you have always wished to be. With this in mind, here's a sneak peek into the daily routine of the successful sigma male.

Note: this list is curated in no specific order. However, take a while to go through all the elements on this list so that you can arrange them to suit your unique situation.

Fix Your Immediate Environment

Something as little as making your bed first thing in the morning can be all the difference you seek in your life. This action has a way of sending signals back to your brain that you are out of bed for the day and not expected to crawl back in. then again, it gives you a sense of accomplishment and order - no matter how little these are.

Set Your Day in Order

Using a to-do list can never go out of style. Once you are done with fixing your immediate environment, the next thing you should do is to have a seat and plan out the activities for your day.

Make a comprehensive list of all the things you should accomplish that day. For one, this gives you a reference point and helps ensure that you don't forget to carry out any important task by the end of the day. Then again, it frees up some space in your mind so that you can focus on other core activities that matter to your life.

Exercise

Work out the kinks in your body from the past day. Then again, exercising doesn't mean that you have to hit the gym, spend 3 hours there, and come out sweating like you barely escaped hell. It simply means that you should carry out the activities that get your blood running for the day.

In a nutshell, work up some sweat and work out the kinks in your joints.

Learn Something New

Another attribute that keeps successful sigma males ahead of the curve is their ability to learn new things every single day. You cannot say that you intend to dominate your world when you are lacking in terms of information.

Commit time every single day to learn something new. This could be in the morning, afternoon, or evening. It could be by reading books, seeing educational shows/documentaries, and listening when you are having conversations with successful people.

In any case, ensure that 24 hours do not pass if you don't learn something new.

Focus on Work

This could be your job, your business, or anything you do that foots the bills. Successful sigma males give their all to the work they do, regardless of what the work is. If you are working for someone else, be committed to it and remember that beyond just working for the person, you are giving yourself a chance to grow as well.

If you are working on your business, see it from the lens of what it can evolve into and not just what it is at the moment. Focus is key when working on achieving anything that is worthy of note in your career.

Minimize Distractions

With the rise of social media and as smartphones become an everyday part of our lives, it is important that you remind yourself to minimize distractions. If you permit social media and the use of your smartphone to eat into the best part of your day, you may be surprised to discover that you wouldn't achieve a lot in the end, regardless of how many hours you put in.

To minimize distractions, put every strategy you can think of in place. Also, remember to reduce the number of hours you spend checking social media every day. For the best results, you can designate time for this task.

Practice Mindfulness and Self-Care

In another chapter of this book, we will delve into the subject of spirituality and how it affects the quality of the sigma male's life. However, it is important that you incorporate self-care practices into your day. Self-care is anything you do as an expression of the fact that you put yourself first. It could be the small things or the grandiose gestures.

Meditation, journaling, and gratitude should be everyday practices.

Quality Sleep

This is where many sigma males tend to miss out. If you don't get quality sleep for any reason, it is only a matter of time until your body betrays you. In a bid to prove that you are goal-driven, do not spend your entire life at work and forget to prioritize your health by sleeping well.

Medical experts advise that adults sleep an average of 8 hours every day. Enjoy your nights.

Appraise Yourself Every Day

At the end of each day, evaluate what you achieved that day and see the things you didn't do well. When you have seen the things you didn't do well, think of what you could have done to make them better and commit to being better as the days pass by.

Self-appraisal is an important attribute of self-made sigma males.

Invest in Building Qualitative Relationships

In subsequent chapters, we'll critically evaluate the subject of managing other people and share tips that can help you to become a pro at this. However, remember that you wouldn't get to the top in isolation. This is why you must invest in building qualitative relationships.

Seek to help people and expect nothing in return. Be nice and don't expect to be appreciated in public. Do good to everybody when the chances present themselves. Remember that you aren't going it for them but that there's karma, and the universe will pay you back in multiples.

Sigma males understand the role of strategic relationships, and they invest time and resources in building these relationships with everything they have in them.

Sniff Out Bad Money Habits and Build Good Ones

We already discussed habits and did justice to the subject of finding out bad habits and how you can eliminate them. One area of your life where you can't afford to deal with bad habits is with respect to your finances.

Commit to developing your money habits every day. This commitment can be expressed in the form of reading some informational finance articles, seeing some minutes of YouTube videos, or just following financial trends every day.

In any case, bad money habits would be the undoing of every sigma male. You do not have that luxury, so you must commit to developing good money habits on time.

Network

Growing social capital is important if you want to reach the zenith of your life, career, and ambitions. To this end, you must make a conscious effort to grow your network every single day. When you get to work, take out some time to meet one new person and have a genuine conversation with them. This would make you lovable and can easily open you up to massive opportunities.

Think Before You Act

To live a successful life as a sigma male, you must develop the capacity to keep your feet on the brakes and think things through before taking any action. Before blowing a gasket and calling your boss out, think about the outcome. Before sending that email, think about what would happen if the email got read.

Thinking and looking before you leap is a life skill you must develop as a sigma male who intends to be successful.

Feed Your Mind with Possibilities

This is where external motivation comes into play. Every day, pick up the story of a successful person you would love to trade places with and read it. In doing things like these, you open yourself up to the lessons you wouldn't have learned otherwise, and this is important if you want to get to the zenith of your life.

Zero Procrastination

If an idea drops into your mind, act on it immediately. The last thing you need is to spend your entire lifetime in analysis paralysis. Taking immediate action is one way to maximize your life and ensure that you accomplish everything you set your mind to do.

Practice Frugality

This applies more to you if you haven't yet become as wealthy as you would like to be (where you can afford anything at all and still have more than enough money to spare). You can't afford to waste money when you are still building your life as a sigma male.

You can afford to live below your means for the moment while you channel your finances toward acquiring assets and growing your net worth.

Make Time to be with the Ones You Love

Family, especially. It is easy to get wrapped up in your quest for success that you forget to show love, care, and attention to the people that would be with you, regardless of what happens.

The successful sigma male understands that family is everything. That is why he makes it a point of duty to just be in the moment when he is with his family. Spend time with your spouse (if you have any), your children, your parents, and your siblings. If you live in the same house with people, ensure they get to see your face every day and feel your presence.

That's one way to enjoy a balanced life as a sigma male.

Stop Being Influenced by External Forces and Begin Your Journey to Self-Mastery

Think of this section as the action plan for this chapter. With the new knowledge you now have, this is how you can begin your journey to self-mastery right now.

Define What Matters to You

To be a true master of yourself, you must know what matters to you. If you don't know what matters to you, you will spend your life on trivial issues. What are your most pressing goals and aspirations at the moment? How would they contribute to the overall look and feel of your life?

Start by making a list of the things that matter to you.

Invest Time and Resources in Conquering Yourself

Everything we will be discussing in this book (plus the ones we have covered so far) is all about self-dominance. It is Plato that said that the first and best victory is the ability to conquer oneself.

It all begins with you.

Understand Your Temperament and Create a Self-Management Plan

We have covered the subject of temperaments in detail. This is where you should get back to that section of this book and define what your own temperaments are. With that information, create a self-management plan that ensures you are still able to live your life to the fullest.

Perfect the Art of Setting Goals

Beyond putting pen to paper, ensure that you create action plans as well. Use the information contained in this chapter of the book to set, pursue, and actualize every goal you have set for yourself.

Work on Your Habits

Ensure that your new habits are in sync with your new identity and the goals you have set for yourself. This is the only way to make sure that you stay on track and become a master of yourself.

Then again, opt-in for accountability because it skyrockets your productivity and efficiency.

Chapter Summary

The journey to becoming a sigma male isn't one that you can treat with levity. If you don't pay close attention to what's happening inside you, you'll soon get frustrated trying to change your external world without any success.

This chapter has covered the foundational principles that you need to be a successful sigma male. Pay attention to all these principles, use the strategies that have been laid out to implement them in your life, and watch how efficient you will become in a matter of time.

Remember, the change you desperately desire begins with you.

Chapter 3: The Sigma Male and His Success Mindset

Can we start this chapter by agreeing on one thing?

Mindset is everything.

You have probably heard this before. You may have even heard it so many times it may even sound like a cliche to you. The thing is, there's nothing cliche about this statement. The first point of contact between the Sigma Male and the successful lifestyle he goes on to lead is his superior mindset.

The sigma male thinks like a boss. He sees life from a completely different point of view. This superior point of view allows him to make strategic decisions, make his best moves even when others do not seem to understand what he is up to, maximize opportunities, and even position himself for much bigger things.

So, as a male who intends to soon become a high-performing sigma male, you must understand the place of having a superior mindset and approaching life from that perspective. In this chapter, we will do adequate justice to that subject.

Understanding the Role of Your Mind in the Formation of Your Beliefs and How Your Beliefs Affect Your Life as a Sigma Male

We already stated in this chapter that most of what you would achieve in your entire life as a sigma male is tied to the quality of your mindset. Before getting any further in this chapter's conversation, it is important that we shed a little light on what mindset truly means (so that we can be on the same page).

Until the 1970s, nothing much was known about the mindset and how it affects every individual. Until that time, humans just knew that they were different, and for some reason, people responded in different ways to the situations life brought their way. Nothing much was said about the reason for these differences until scientists and behavioral experts rolled up their sleeves and got to work.

The first real definition and explanation of the word came from a psychologist called Carol Dweck. Her study began in a rather unconventional way when it struck her that children could look every inch alike (as is the case with identical twins) but still have contrasting responses to the same situation. This revelation sparked up her curiosity, and Carol began digging deeper into the cause of these differences in behavior.

At first, she was intrigued by the fact that children responded to danger in different ways. On one end of the pendulum, there were children who actively sought to be put in situations where they had to deal with challenges. These children were usually confrontational, never afraid of a fight, and they were usually the leaders of every gang they belonged to. On the other hand, there was this category of children who would do everything to never be caught up in a brawl. They hated attention, disliked the idea of having a faceoff, and would do anything to avoid running into a challenge from anywhere. These children, she discovered, were mostly the ones who stayed in the background but were mostly the brains behind every successful operation.

These findings spurred her into taking a tour of how the mind works. She discovered a lot of intriguing facts and began to teach those who cared to listen to what she had to say at the time (although she was mostly rejected because of the novelty of her ideas).

Her work would later form the basis of all that has been modified and taught in modern-day science as the concept of a person's mindset.

Simply put, mindset is the set of beliefs that shape the way you see and interact with the world around you. It covers how you feel, think, and behave when you are exposed to different situations every day. Your mindset is the result of everything that has happened to you during the course of your entire lifetime. It results from the experiences you have had, the people that have had access to your space, the conversations you constantly engage in, and even the things you say to yourself/others say to you.

There will be no mindset if you haven't had any experiences in your life.

At first, people used to think that one's mindset was absolute; that is, a person's mindset couldn't be altered once it was fixed. However, the studies of Carol Dweck unraveled this belief and revealed to the entire world that it is possible for a person to commit themselves to constant evolution such that they can identify limiting mindsets and, with the right actions, change these mindsets immediately.

Her study brought about what is known today as "growth mindset" and "fixed mindset," which are the 2 main types of mindsets everyone has. Let's take a quick look at each of them.

Fixed Mindset

A fixed mindset is one in which the person believes that everything they hold dear in their minds is absolute and cannot be changed. A person with a fixed mindset believes that they are naturally good at something or not. As far as they are concerned, there are no middle grounds, and they have absolutely no hopes of learning any new skill when they have identified that they do not have the natural propensity for that skill.

The major challenge with having a fixed mindset is that you'd soon be left behind in every sense of the word. You'll come to a point in your life, relationships, career, and business where you would need to learn new things, adapt, and evolve. Since you haven't yet thought that it is possible to learn and grow on the job, you would find yourself stuck and lacking the motivation to commit yourself to any kind of learning.

It is important to note that the sigma male who believes that he is meant for the top has little or nothing to do with a fixed mindset. Even if you find yourself with one, it is up to you to commit to changing it and evolving into a growth mindset.

Growth Mindset

This is the "I can do it all" mindset of champions. A person with a growth mindset understands that life is a gift, and they have a responsibility to make the most out of their lives. Hence, they approach every situation/scenario with a sense of optimism.

As opposed to a person with a fixed mindset, this person commits more time to learn, evolve, and grow with the times. He understands that he has a role to play in how his life eventually pans out. Hence, he would do anything to ensure that he keeps evolving.

His language is "I may not have this skill now. However, with the right amount of determination, commitment, and diligence, I can pick up this skill in record time." A man with a growth mindset can accomplish any task he sets himself up to do because he is always obsessed with the "how can I accomplish this" question.

To be successful in life as a sigma male, you must adopt a growth mindset in every facet of your life. This should cut across your career, business, relationships, and even your personal life. If you do not have a growth mindset, the challenges that life throws at you will eventually bring you to a screeching stop when you get to the end of your abilities.

How to Shift from a Fixed Mindset to a Growth Mindset

Now that we have identified what both are and the classical differences between all two, here are some ways to move from having a fixed mindset to having a growth mindset.

Identify the Need for Change

It is impossible to commit yourself to fix a problem when you haven't yet admitted its existence. If you don't first admit that you have a fixed mindset, you will never take the steps needed to move you to the place where you have a growth mindset.

Keep Failure in Perspective

The chances are that as a sigma male on his way to a successful future, you will come across many failures. It is important to keep this at the back of your mind as you go about your daily activities.

Failure is not the end of the road. When things do not happen as planned, take them in stride and move on with your life. The first step to having a growth mindset is to see failure as an integral part of success.

Avoid Negative Self-Talk

What are the things you say to yourself when you are all by yourself? Do you use empowering words, or do you always talk down on yourself? If you do the former, you would be stuck for a long time because the words you say to yourself go a long way in determining the quality of your life as a sigma male.

One sure way to transition from having a fixed mindset to a growth mindset is by focusing on using powerful words on yourself. Many people call this "the use of affirmations," and in subsequent chapters, we will go all into this subject.

Seek Constructive Criticism

One way to veer off course is by opening your ears and your mind to everyone around you. The fact that people are in your space shouldn't automatically mean that you would give them access to say the things that you listen to. So, another way to move from having a fixed mindset is by taking criticism only from the right source.

Prequalify the people you lend your ears to. If you want to have a successful life as a sigma male, ensure that you take constructive criticism only. And when you have gotten the action points from these, commit to putting all that you have learned to good use.

Celebrate the Work You are Putting In

It is easy to set goals and get lost in the pursuit of goals that we fail to celebrate ourselves for just showing up and doing so well. The challenge with this is that if you keep your eyes focused on the goal and forget to celebrate the work you are putting in, you rob yourself of the opportunity to experience true happiness every single day.

So, if you are taking steps to be a better man every day and you are consciously working toward the actualization of your goals, celebrate all that effort you are putting in.

Because you are already killing it.

Remind Yourself of the Immense Power of Your Brain

Neuroplasticity is one concept that can change your entire idea of a fixed mindset within the shortest possible time. By consciously reminding yourself that your mind can always readjust to fit new frames, you open yourself up to learn new things and enjoy the world every single day.

When you feel overwhelmed, pat yourself on the back and be reminded that you can handle anything that life throws your way.

Then again, every other thing we would discuss in this book is geared toward helping you live the best life you can possibly imagine. By applying the principles covered in this book, you open yourself up to truly function with a growth mindset.

Common Mindset Blocks In Different Areas of Your Life

Here are some of the mindset configurations that are wrong. You may have had them forever, but the first step to being rid of them is to start by identifying their presence consciously and committing to refrain from holding on to them after identifying their existence.

Mindset blocks in different areas of your personal life include:

1. You never feel qualified for anything, no matter how qualified you actually are.

The downside of this mindset block is that you never get around to achieving anything worthwhile in your life. Since you believe that you are never qualified for anything, you would always shortchange yourself under the guise of being humble.

Soon enough, you may even begin to deal with deep-seated feelings of self-hate when you look around to discover that time has passed and you haven't yet accomplished all the things you said you will.

2. You maximize every decision and feel like making one slip-up will ruin your entire life.

While it is important to lead a cautious life, you must also remind yourself to approach life with the knowledge that you have to take a few risks every once in a while if you want to make the most out of life.

Getting out of bed every day is a risk. Catching the train and riding to work is a huge risk. For one, the train could veer off course and plunge you into your death. So, if you believe that one slip-up can ruin your entire life, you may find yourself under the pressure of leading a picture-perfect life. The result is that you may just end up not being able to achieve anything worthwhile.

Maximize your decisions, yes. However, do not let a fear of making mistakes strip you of the opportunity to make the most of life.

3. You want to move on to the next level but feel like you are standing in your own way.

This is the daily chant of men who feel like they are constantly in a vicious cycle of self-sabotage. Every time they are on the brink of a major breakthrough, they do something to ruin everything they have worked so hard for.

They mess up at work a few days to when they should be picked up for a promotion. They consciously decide to come late for a presentation when they know their pitch would be the best. They refuse to sit for their exams because they know their results would be the best.

Always feeling like you are standing in your own way is one of the worst things that can happen in your life. This is because when you feel like you are the cause of the challenges you are going through, it will take a lot of self-examination to get to the cause of the challenge and start work on fixing what has been broken.

4. You feel like making extra money will replace the stress you feel right now, or everything will snap into place when you make extra cash from your job or business.

What if we tell you that you do not need extra money to be successful? What if you were told right now that what you need isn't (necessarily) a salary raise or a fatter bank account? What if we say to you that what you need to be successful is a better relationship with money?

Money hardly takes the stress away from our lives. As a matter of fact, the richer you get, the more chances that more stress will come to you. For one, people will come to beg you for money. You will have bigger responsibilities.

So, no! You don't need more money to decide to let go of stress and just enjoy the life you are living at the moment. Focus on developing stronger money habits and getting financial intelligence. When you are done, start thinking of how to scale your earnings.

Then again, you can commit to enjoying your life as a sigma male, regardless of how many dollars you earn per month.

5. You feel like you are not good enough and should step out of the way for more deserving people to enjoy life.

This also relates to the point buttressed in number 1. You don't have to step aside for anyone to feel good about themselves. Whoever is qualified has all they need to enjoy their lives while you do the same as well.

6. You say yes to everything and everyone, even if doing that affects your mental health or makes you make unnecessary compromises in your life.

"This is because I am a 'good' man and must give my all to make sure that the people around me have their lives figured out."

If this sounds like the conversations you have with yourself, you may want to start with taking some lessons on self-confidence. You don't have to say yes to everything and everyone, especially if they go against your personal beliefs and convictions. You don't have to be uncomfortable in a bid to make the next person feel good about themself.

7. You are terribly critical.

This sense of criticism shows up when you make a mistake, don't hit the goals you set for yourself, or when someone else around you makes a mistake. The mindset change you should adopt here is to remind yourself that everyone makes mistakes every once in a while.

So, instead of spending your entire life trying to avoid mistakes and criticizing yourself and others when these things happen, focus on finding remedies and moving on with your life.

8. You always imagine things going bad.

This could be the result of past negative experiences you've had that left you feeling sad and out of it. If it is easier for you to imagine bad things happening to you, you may want to start by revisiting your past so that you can clearly identify the experiences that leave you feeling the way you do.

9. You feel depressed every time something happens.

This can also be directly traced back to a traumatizing experience you have had in the past. If you always feel triggered and feel like you are coming to the end of yourself, whenever you are faced with a specific scenario, your first job is to unpack what happened to you so that you can better understand your emotions and draft an exit route for yourself.

10. You feel like your partner is doing you a favor by being with you.

You may not be able to maximize true love if this is the way you feel about yourself. No. they aren't doing you a favor by being with you. They have seen the good in you, they love you, and they have decided to be in a committed relationship with you.

11. You feel like you are doing your partner a favor by being with them.

There's no relationship that can thrive if either of the parties involved feels like they are doing the other a favor by being in a relationship with them. If this is the way you feel about your partner, you will end up making them beg and grovel for crumbs of the love and attention you should be showering them with.

Relationships aren't about who is doing the other person a favor. They are about love, mutual respect, and honest feelings from both sides.

12. You think your children won't respect you if you aren't a strict father.

This is the reason why many men have gone out of their way to make sure that their children see them as hard men that can be respected. They allow themselves to fall into the pit hole of being frigid and even refrain from allowing themselves to have strong and healthy relationships with their children.

To correct this mindset, remind yourself that you can have a strong, healthy relationship with your children and get them to respect you even while they still see you as their closest friend.

How to Identify Limiting Mindsets and Eliminate Them from Your Life

The last section of this chapter has covered 12 common limiting mindsets that you may have right now. The first step to correcting limiting mindsets is to get out of your bubble and admit the presence of these limiting mindsets immediately.

As we already said, there's no hope of fixing a problem you don't yet believe exists. So, to fix limiting mindsets, just follow the steps we discussed when we talked about moving from a fixed mindset to a growth mindset.

Follow all 6 steps and focus on making every day much better than the last.

Chapter Summary

1. Everything begins with the mind. One of the key secrets every successful sigma male has is that they do not joke with their minds. They understand the power of having superior beliefs, so they do all they can to ensure that the thoughts they always think about are empowering and positive.
2. Everyone in the world has either a growth mindset or a fixed mindset. No one has none of them. Then again, it is possible to switch from having a fixed mindset to a growth mindset.
3. To switch mindsets, simply follow the 6 steps we discussed in this chapter of the book. If you commit to it over a period, you will even notice the changes in your personal life and also come to see how much this activity will give you a sense of control over your life.

Chapter 4: Hypnosis, Empathy, and Psychic Abilities

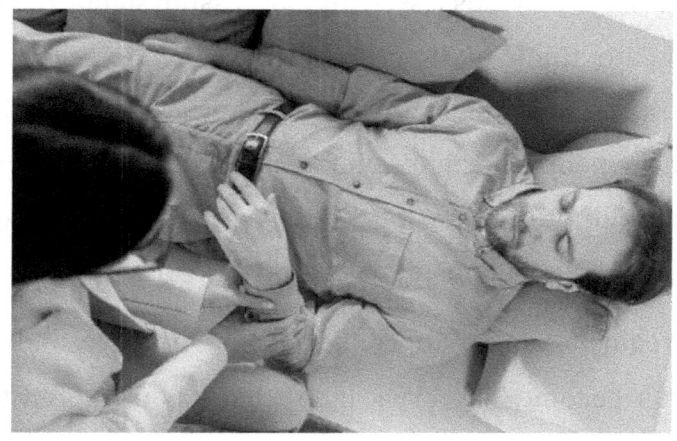

Have you ever met another man that has an inexplicable ability over others? You step into a room, and they are the center of attention. Even without doing a lot of work, it feels like they are the ones calling the shots in that room.

For some unexplainable reason, it feels like these men are black holes. Everything in the room exists because they are. People bask when they turn their attention to them. They call the shots. Everyone wants to impress them. It can be scary.

You know what's worse than this/ being in proximity with these kinds of people. When you engage them in conversations, it feels like your mouth develops a mind of its own. Your brain short-circuits. You find yourself saying only the things they would approve of, and this inordinate desire to be approved by them creeps up and takes over your conscious thoughts.

This is another skill possessed by successful sigma males. Some people like to think of it as being psychic. However, it is the coagulation of a ton of skills they have. They are able to wield these skills to make people become comfortable around them. In addition, with these skills, it is easier for them to get the trust of people, gain attention, and have people move in a certain direction.

With the requisite amount of consciousness, practice, and diligence, you too can become "the black hole" that has mastered the art of connecting with people subconsciously. This is one powerful way to increase your influence in every scenario. Focus on harnessing these skills.

Chapter 4 of this book will show you just how. We will also help you coordinate your activities so you don't dabble in less-than-good stuff in your bid to develop your powers of empathy.

Hypnosis and What This Truly Means

If you have seen the movies where hypnosis is represented, you most likely have a negative interpretation of hypnosis. Close your eyes and think about it for one second.

Here's what (most likely) crossed your mind.

A bespectacled man is sitting on a couch with a wry smile on his face. Across from where he's seated, there's a glass-eyes lady sitting on a couch as well. Her eyes are wide and unfocused as she responds to everything he says. He snaps his hands, and she jerks in fear. He gives ridiculous instructions, and she responds immediately without hesitation.

Well, this is mostly the picture the media has painted when it comes to hypnosis. The thing is, while there may be some elements of truth in this (you can get people to behave in a certain way when you apply the principle of hypnosis), it isn't entirely true. Hypnosis is an age-long practice that has been used for many different reasons. Here are some of them.

1. **Hypnosis can be turned inwards:** It can be used to help you gain control over behaviors that you do not like. So, if you master how to use it in this regard, you can use it to get out of terrible habits that you have picked up over time.
2. **Hypnosis can also be used to cope with anxiety, depression, and pain:** The principles taught in hypnosis can

be used to deal with intense grief and help you gain control over your life after you have been ravaged by things like these.
3. **People who have issues with sleep can be trained to deal with these using hypnotism:** Challenges like insomnia, sleepwalking, or intense anxiety that keeps them from enjoying a good night's sleep can be trained to relax and improve their sleep habits using practices of hypnotism.
4. **Hypnotism can be used in medicine and wellness:** When deployed in this regard, it can come in handy in the management of weight, reduction of the chances that a person will become obese, and also in managing other chronic health issues like hypertension and stress disorders.

So, can we start by agreeing that hypnotism isn't all bad as you may have thought before now? Since we have that out of the way, let us look at what hypnotism is all about.

Hypnosis (also known as Hypnotherapy or Hypnotic suggestion) is a trance-like state wherein the person undergoing hypnosis has increased focus, and all their senses are heightened. Hypnosis is usually done under the watchful eyes of an experienced therapist who does this using specific repeated phrases and mental imagery. The aim of these is to get the recipient to feel relaxed, become more open to suggestions, or use hypnotism as a tool to achieve an intended aim like effecting some psychological changes and handling health conditions like obesity.

It is worthy of note that hypnotism isn't all bad. As a matter of fact, hypnotism is a technique that you should try using on yourself first because it helps you gain mastery over yourself and increases the chances that you will become the sigma male you have always wanted to be. In addition to these, hypnosis comes in handy when you are trying to deal with issues relating to mental health and stability. This makes it one effective remedy for stress, anxiety, depression, and even suicidal thoughts.

While it is great to point out all the good parts of hypnosis, it is also important to note that it doesn't come without its fair share of downsides. For one, if hypnosis is conducted without the supervision of a skilled and competent therapist, it could easily go south because the process involves reprogramming a person's mind, sometimes to extremes.

In addition, here are some of the identified side effects that can accompany hypnosis. While these aren't common, we cannot rule off the fact that these signs are possible, especially when hypnotism goes wrong (that is, when a skilled and competent therapist doesn't oversee the entire process). Some side effects include:

1. Anxiety and distress
2. Malaise
3. Intense headache
4. Drowsiness
5. Creation of false memories and daydreaming

As mentioned early on, hypnotism should first be used on you so that you can become a master of yourself. Let us quickly take a look at how to use this skill positively on yourself.

How to Turn Hypnosis Inwards in a Positive Way

Let us take a quick look at how you can use hypnosis on yourself to achieve the positive things you have always wanted in your life. Remember, this technique can be used to achieve many goals like getting yourself primed for weight loss, putting yourself in the mental state to be super productive at work, or getting your body to loosen up after an intense day of stress and anxiety.

Here are the steps you must follow to use hypnosis on yourself first.

You Should Be Comfy

You wouldn't want to get into that state of deep concentration, only to be interrupted by an intense desire to get up and scratch your balls. Prevent this from the start by ensuring that everything you have on your body and around you (at the moment, at least) contributes to making you feel comfortable.

For the best results, you may want to consider wearing your nightwear or at least being in a pair of loose drawstring pants. This way, you mitigate the chances of being interrupted mid-session.

Starched, stiff, tight clothing should get off. If that's all you have (for some reason), then consider doing this naked. Also, put your gadgets away or silence them if they must be near you during this exercise.

Be in the Right Spot

It is best to try this method if you are alone. It wouldn't be much of an issue to practice self-hypnosis if you are a bachelor who lives alone. If you have others who live with you, it might be profitable to bring them up to speed before you start the entire process. If you aren't comfortable telling them the exact thing you are up to, consider just letting them know that you will be busy for the next few minutes and would appreciate it if they refrain from trying to distract you.

Afterward, prepare the spot you would use for this exercise. Try laying out a mat (a yoga mat, if you have one) on the spot you would use. When you are about to get seated, remember to be in a position that supports your back because you may be here for a while, and you don't want to put your body through undue stress at the end of the day.

Know Why You are About to Do This

One of the reasons why many men get into the act of self-hypnosis and end up having nothing to show for it is because they get into the arena without exact goals. What in the world do you seek to achieve with these hypnosis sessions? Can you write down an exact goal you want to achieve (using the SMART criteria we already discussed)?

Whatever it is, you increase your chances of achieving something tangible if you get into these sessions knowing the exact thing you want to achieve.

Focus Your Eyes on a Point

The principle of self-hypnosis revolves around your ability to focus all your energies on one single thing. This begins with what you do with your eyes.

At the beginning of this exercise, find one thing within your line of sight (like a specific flower in its vase or a book on your bookshelf). Conversely, you can make the focus exercise easier by lighting a candle, placing it across from where you are seated, and focusing on its flame as the candle diminishes.

Note, however, that whatever you choose to focus on should be in a place where looking at it doesn't make your body uncomfortable. This is to say that your focus object should be on the same eye level as you.

Take Deep Breaths

Now that you are in a perfect position and you have chosen a focus object, the next step is to start deep breaths. Start with breathing in from your nose. Hold the air in your lungs for a few seconds and gently release that gust of air from your mouth.

While taking in your breaths, ensure you fill up your lungs before holding on and letting go of the air through your mouth. As you do these, keep your eyes focused on your target and imagine that with each successful breath, your eyelids are becoming heavier (like someone who is being overcome by the desire to sleep).

As you keep doing this, your eyelids would begin getting heavy. A time will come when it would be impossible to keep them open any longer.

Don't fight this!

Don't Stop the Process

Even when it is almost impossible to keep your eyelids open, continue the process. One thing you'd notice when your eyes slip shut is that your senses have become more heightened. The second you close your eyes, your mind would latch onto the deep breaths you are taking. You'll literally hear yourself sucking in those breaths. You would hear your heartbeat, and you may even feel your hearing stretching out to cover other parts of the room you are seated in.

If this happens to you, just know that you are right on track.

Note, also, that your mind may attempt to veer off course every once in a while. When this happens, return your attention to your breathing and continue the process.

Include the Visualization Process

Up until now, you have focused on clearing your mind and just focusing on your breaths. You've had no mental picture before you, and that's the entire plan. However, this is the time to step things up a notch. It is time to let your mind start painting the pictures of an ideal place.

With your eyes closed and your focus on the deep breaths you are still sucking in, open your mind up to pictures of what the ideal situation you want to attain looks like.

Would you like to shed some weight? Imagine yourself in beach shorts and with washboard abs; not ashamed to prance around in nothing but your beachwear because you have attained the body structure you have been gunning for.

Do you like to have some extra cash in your bank account? Imagine the feeling of joy and the smile on your face when you whip your phone out and check your bank statement, only to see that you have struck that amount of money you set out to save.

Do you want to stop a bad habit? Imagine the amount of productivity and freedom that would come with knowing that you no longer have to struggle with that bad habit.

The idea here is to imagine yourself in the ideal scenario you want to be in, and so, the list goes on.

Take Some Time to 'Feel'

One of the major reasons why you may spend a lot of time in this state and not achieve anything at the end of the hypnosis exercise is that you are always in a hurry to exit this activity. The longer you stay in this state, the more vivid your imagination becomes. To make the most out of these exercises, aim at spending as much time as possible in this state.

When you have gotten the exact picture from step 7, take some time to feel yourself in that state. If you see yourself in a different location, just give yourself the time to appreciate the colors of the sky and the song of the nearby birds (if any). If you have imagined yourself in a lither body, take some time to feel the strength coursing through your calves as you run down the beach or walk around. Just do all you can to add feelings and emotions to the pictures floating around your head.

The idea behind this is to cause an emotional connection between your body and what is currently going on in your mind. That's the way to ensure that you jumpstart the process of getting that result as fast as possible.

Speak

This is the time to lend your voice to the overall experience you are having. After feeling whatever you felt from the last point, give the experience more meaning by speaking about it. For the best results, use short, powerful mantras like "I am at peace."

Speaking at this stage gives a deeper meaning to the hypnotism exercise.

Zero into Your Goal

You know how you open up a picture and zoom in, right? This is exactly what you want to achieve at this stage of the hypnotism exercise. After coming up with a vivid picture and speaking about whatever you are seeing, it is time to zero in on the tiniest details of the goal you set out to achieve from the beginning. At this stage, you want to be as detailed as possible.

See yourself already living in the reality of the goal you set out to achieve. At the same time, do not forget to also focus on controlling your breath.

Deep breaths still!

Affirm

This goes beyond just using mantras. At this stage, you want to be more specific about the words you use. So, if you set out to shed some extra pounds, this is the part where you affirm that you have hit your desired weight. Remain in this state for the next 7 minutes even as you keep affirming your goal. When you are done, it is time to return to normal.

To return back to the way you were in the beginning, simply imagine that with each breath you take, you are drawing in energy from the world surrounding you. Also, imagine that each time you exhale, you are sending the energy you have drawn in straight to your core. Do this for the next 5 minutes as you carefully allow your body to start taking note of the world around you once again. At the end of about 5 minutes, gently pry your eyes open and get ready to stand up.

You may want to take it easy as you have been in a trance-like state forever. If you force your body into moving abruptly, you may end up causing more damage to yourself. So, stay in the seated position until you feel it is safe to move your body. If any parts of your body feel like they have been put to sleep, simply flex that part of your body until the blood flow returns there.

Count down from 20. By the time you get to 0, you should be good and ready to hit the roads once again.

A Few Things to Note About Self-Hypnosis

1. Do not expect that after 1 or 2 sessions, everything will return to normal (that is, that you will hit the desired state you want to hit). This isn't feasible considering that you are trying to

correct what took you years to form. The magic of self-hypnosis comes from your ability to be consistent and stick to the game over a long period.

If it takes 2 months of consistency to hit your desired target, then so be it.

2. The first few times, self-hypnosis will be awkward. You may even feel like laughing at yourself at the beginning. That's absolutely fine. Then again, if you feel frustrated because you cannot seem to control your mind well, that's also absolutely fine.

Gaining better control of your mind and trance-like states comes with practice. In summary, everything will get better with time and consistent practice.

3. As much as possible, do not get into self-hypnosis without seeking the guidance of a behavioral expert. Before you start with self-hypnosis, please do all you can to talk to your therapist as they have what it takes to see things from an advanced point of view and offer you expert guidance on how to make the most out of self-hypnosis.

If there's one thing you should have seen by now, it is that self-hypnosis has more to do with you than any other person, right? Now that you have cracked the code of how to transform your life with self-hypnosis techniques, can we talk about the next life-changing principle that can help you attain all you want in life?

Empathy: Does It Always Equate To Weakness?

If history is any indication, the chances are that you may have met those people (males especially) who, for some reason, have this skewed ideology that you have to be closed-off, snooty, and arrogant to get people to take you seriously. As far as these men are concerned, there's absolutely no way that you can be a nice guy and have the people in your world respect you.

So, they do their best to come off as intimidating.

These guys could be anybody. They could be your dad, boss at work, an elder sibling, or the random neighbor that you run into once in a blue moon.

What's worse s that if you take a close look at them, it feels like what they believe works out fine for them. You see their children respecting them and their spouses taking their words as law. You see their colleagues (or subordinates) at work deferring to them, and it just feels like they always have their way.

This can leave you wondering. "Are their beliefs right?"

So, here's the thing. It is not easy to tell whether or not what they believe is working perfectly for them. This is because, at first glance, many of these men look like they've got their lives figured out. It feels like everything is working well for them. However, a couple of them would tell you (in their unguarded moments) what life truly feels like. You may end up hearing a couple of them saying that they wished they could turn back some things. You may even hear the pain in their voices and see how lonely they have become over time.

So, if you intend to lead a life where the people in your world love/value you, but you do not want to intimidate or coerce people to respect you, if you would also love to build deep connections with the people that matter to you, you want to take empathy seriously.

Before we proceed, let's answer the question already.

No! If done well, empathy doesn't always equate to weakness. As a matter of fact, it may even be a sign of immense strength.

That said, what then is empathy, and how can you use it to your good as a sigma male?

Wikipedia defines empathy as the ability to identify or feel what another person feels from within their frame of reference. Simply put, it is the ability to put yourself in the shoes of another person, so you can identify with them when they are going through something (usually some hard times).

As simple as they may seem, a lot of people do not have the skills of being empathic toward the people in their world. The sad thing is that if you lack empathy, it can easily be said of you that you are callous, mean, or cold-hearted (and all those wouldn't be a lie from the standpoint of other people). One of the first things to note about empathy is that it is one social skill that makes you endearing almost instantly., if you can communicate with someone who may be going through hard times in their life and make them feel as though you understand exactly why they feel the way they do, they'd get more comfortable around you.

When this happens, you will discover how easy it is to have people on your side. When you make someone feel seen, loved, and heard when they desperately want to, there's every possibility that you will have them on your side for a long time to come.

Take this as one of the main secrets of life. If you can get close enough to the stakeholders of anything, communicate empathy when they desperately need it, and let them see that you want nothing in return (except to be of genuine help to them), you are already light years ahead of any other person who may try to get in your way when the time for those people you communicated empathy towards to make decisions that concern and affect you.

Communicating empathy at work is one sure way to keep your career on an upward and forward trajectory for a long time. For empathy to work for you, you have to figure out exactly how you can use it to get people on your side. To accomplish that, follow the steps we are about to discuss right now.

How To Improve Your Empathic Skills And Make Them Work For You

Understand Context

There are times when you are better off not trying to communicate empathy toward a person. This could be a colleague at work or any random stranger you meet. Before deciding to get close to someone and helping them get through some hard times, take a step back to analyze the situation.

Can your acts of kindness be misinterpreted? Can your goodness be taken with a pinch of salt? Can your empathy be mistaken for something that would cost you a lot in the future?

Will your acts of empathy cause you mental stress, physical harm, or excessive emotional drainage? If this is the case, please take a step back and allow things to ride out themselves. After all, you aren't going to be able to save the entire world, no matter how hard you try.

Expose Yourself to New Experiences

It is almost impossible to fake empathy for a scenario that is 100% new to you. When you just can't relate with a person on a level, you just can't. If you try to present a front that you can, they'll see through your act and call everything you have done BS. To prevent this from happening, constantly expose yourself to novel experiences.

The next time you walk into a room where intellectual conversations are going on, know when to keep mute and just listen to others share from their depths of experience. Again, one sure way to ensure that you can relate with people from this point of honesty is by reading fictional books.

Before you reject this notion, research has shown that when people read fictional works, their brains feel like they have just entered new worlds and experiences. Then again, one of the beautiful things about exposing yourself to fictional work is that you are taken on a tour of the character's mind. You experience their internal battles, see from their perspective, and you may even catch yourself trying to rationalize their decisions throughout that book.

Without your knowledge, this helps you to build your powers of empathy. Because you have now seen them from the inside, it becomes easier to relate with people who have similarities to them.

Don't Be Biased When You Listen to People

We are all born in different situations. Our experiences make us form different beliefs, and even without our complete consent, we may find ourselves expressing some level of bias against a person, group, scenario, or thing.

While this is difficult to admit, it is important to note that there is hardly a person on earth who doesn't have some kind of biases lodged somewhere in their mind.

Another way to harness your empathic skills is to teach yourself how to listen more than you speak. The next time you get into conversations with people, do not just be the only one talking and don't always seek to be right. Sometimes, keep your mouth shut, encourage the other person to speak up while you listen to them, and try to see things from their perspective.

Being less biased against people or situations makes it easier to communicate with you. This, in turn, is one sure way to improve your empathy levels.

Make Efforts to Comfort People

All the empathy in the world will do you no good if the person you are expressing that empathy to doesn't know what you are trying to do because you never expressed yourself to them.

The next time you are with someone who's crying, try to help them feel better. This could be in the form of thoughtful comments, a towel for them to wipe their tears, or a small hug (when the situation feels right).

When people know that they can be comfortable around you, they are more likely to open up to you, and this gives you an edge in their lives as they become favorably disposed towards you.

Thoughtful Actions Always Win

This goes beyond a lousy attempt at saying 'sorry' when someone is crying. It speaks of something bigger and much better. Little actions of thoughtfulness always win. To different people, there are different things that matter. If you are able to decode those things and do them, you become the person's favorite almost immediately.

These little things could be replacing the flowers on your boss' desk every day you report to work, greeting the 'inconsequential' secretary with a huge smile on your face every day you report for work, or even just offering your workmates a bowl of cookies every once in a while.

These little actions make you endearing to the people in your world. When the chips are down, you wouldn't just be loved by the people that matter. You would also be one of the first people to be considered every time there's a need for someone to be promoted or for better opportunities to be released to a couple of you.

Apply this principle in your relationships, personal life, and in every other place you meet and interact with people, even in your place of worship (if you have one). These acts of empathy will place you leagues ahead of every other person around you.

Harnessing and Deploying Your Psychic Abilities as a Sigma Male

Now that we have gone over the fundamental concepts of empathy and self-hypnosis, this is how to harness and deploy your psychic abilities to get you the results you seek in different scenarios.

Before we do that, let us take a quick look at the concept of the 4 clairs (as they form a major part of psychic abilities).

Clairaudience

Simply put, this is the psychic ability to hear voices. Let go of the deep breath you just took in right now. You wouldn't hear strange, scary voices (in most cases) unless you have been previously diagnosed with some psychological conditions and severe hormonal imbalance).

Usually, these voices sound like someone is speaking in your mind. Most times, you would hear them sound like your own voice, but the clear difference between Clairaudience and your random thoughts is the fact that when you want to trace the root of the ideas that came from Clairaudience, you will discover that nothing about those ideas came from you.

They are usually superior to your regular thoughts, more precise in communication, and are as clear as day when they come.

One simple way to develop clairaudience is by opening up your intuition and letting go of the fear of the unknown. Focus on the good that can come to you when you approach life from this plane of precision.

Clairvoyance

This is the ability to see images or look beyond what your physical eyes can see. These images usually come as flashes and can sometimes be interpreted as 'visions.' However, they are mostly presented as metaphors and can give you a lot of insight into what is happening in the life of a person at every given time.

For example, a clairvoyant message for a person dealing with stress and overwhelm can present itself as a picture of that person struggling under heavy weight or as a picture of the ground beneath their feet rumbling like the first few minutes before an earthquake.

To develop clairvoyance, you just need to be more mindful of what goes on in your mind. Are there those images that pop into your mind from nowhere? Do not just brush them off and treat them with levity, especially if there was no context to those thoughts and images. Pay attention, as it may be your subconscious' way of giving you some much-desired intel.

Claircognizance

This is the psychic ability that manifests itself as 'just knowing.' If you possess this, you take a quick look at people, and you just seem to know things about them, things they haven't talked to you about.

When this psychic ability is at work, you tend to decode complex information about a person without giving it much thought. It happens within a split second. One second you are exposed to the person, and the next second, something about them just snaps into place in your mind.

With claircognizance, you can tell a lot about a person you have just met. When used well, this psychic ability can open you up to people who you wouldn't have been able to access if you didn't have it. However, when abused, you can get yourself some enemies with this psychic ability. It is all about context and knowing when to let some intel you receive from your intuition just slide.

To develop claircognizance, simply tap into the powers of your intuition and subconscious mind. The next time you come across a subject that keeps you stumped and makes you feel helpless, take a deep breath and ask your intuition to help you out.

You may just be pleasantly surprised at what will come out of this little experiment, especially as you begin to give more space for your mind and intuition to step in and help you on a regular basis.

Clairsentience

This is simply the ability to recognize feelings. Generally speaking, clairsentience is the most common of all 4 clairs. This is because almost everyone has been in that position where we are able to recognize feelings.

You walk into a room and feel the collective energy in the place. You talk to someone, and you can feel when they are lying to you. Your guts take over at specific times, and you can just feel danger, even when there are no obvious reasons for feeling that way.

When this Clair is at work in you, it is easier to interact with people and understand them at a deep level. This is because sometimes, your body may even begin to respond to theirs. This establishes a deep-seated bond almost immediately.

To develop clairsentience, take extra care to note down your feelings. Whenever you feel something strongly, do not brush it under the carpet and assume that all is well. Jot them down. After an appreciable amount of time has passed, take a look at the journal where you have been preserving those messages, and you may be amazed at how often your sense of clairsentience has been working.

Developing Cutting-Edge Self-Confidence By Using Self-Hypnosis

The central idea behind this chapter so far has been to debunk the myths associated with psychism. One thing you should know at this time is that when psychism is spoken about, it doesn't have to be in terms of negative things.

In an earlier section, we already talked about how to turn hypnosis inwards. The technique to develop insane levels of self-confidence as a sigma male by using the skills of self-hypnotism is the same as the way you would use it to work on anything else.

Simply set your goal (which would be to become a confident sigma male who isn't afraid of going after what he wants and deserves). When the time for visualization comes, think about the effects that having a strong sense of self-esteem will have on you and see yourself living in that reality already.

Do this over an extended period of time and combine all the strategies covered in this bible. Watch how confident and self-assured you'd become after a significant amount of time.

Chapter Summary

1. Psychism isn't all bad. If used well, it is a powerful way of taking control of yourself and producing mind-blowing results in your life as a sigma male.

2. Hypnosis isn't all about casting a zombie spell on people and getting them to take specific harmful actions. As a matter of fact, when used well, you should focus on using it to make your life better first. Craft yourself into becoming the sigma male you have always desired to be by harnessing your hypnotism skills for yourself.
3. There are 4 Clairs that affect how we interact with ourselves and the people in our world. Clairvoyance, Clairsentience, Clairaudience, and Claircognizance. To lead an extraordinary life as a sigma male, you need all 4 of them.

The best part is that you can develop these senses. Use the strategies detailed in this chapter to develop yours, and you'd soon become more desirable to the people around you.

Chapter 5: Body Language for Strategic Communication

Do you know what speaks louder than your voice?

"Action," they say.

However, what if there's something that has a voice that is just as loud as your actions?

This is where body language comes to play.

For the longest time, not many people understood the connection between body language and communication. For some reason, everyone knew that you could tell a lot about a person from the way they carry themselves and how they respond to life with parts of their body, but not many people had figured out the method to that madness.

All these started changing in the 4th century in Ancient Greece. Around that time, it was easy to know a lot about a man simply by looking at how he walked. Noblemen and those from wealthy/influential homes walked in a way that was uncharacteristically cocky and far-fetched to ordinary men. Nobles were easily recognizable by their long and sure strides. They held their heads up, squared their shoulders, and had a habit of looking people in the eyes when they talked to them. Their handshakes were firm, and every time you saw them, they most likely had confident smiles on their faces.

On the other end of the pendulum, the lowly ones stayed at the mercy of whatever society decided to let them have. The drop in their shoulders when they walked suggested that they had been weighed down by the immense burdens many of them had to bear. They could barely look anyone they considered to be superior in their faces, and they always scurried around when they walked (just like scared mice running away from the treacherous hands of a cat).

Regardless of the disguise in place, it was always easy to tell the rich/influential apart from the poor/lowly within a few seconds. This wasn't only endemic to ancient Greece as other parts of the world began to have these people represented in their communities.

The study of body language began to be modified from there. As modern-day medicine and science came around, many scientists and behavioral experts isolated the subject of body language and began to explain it from the context of the 21st-century world.

One of the first differences between the primitive idea of body language and how it is understood in today's world is the fundamental belief that body language isn't a global construct but is largely dependent on societal context and values. This implies that what can be seen as respect in Central America can easily be interpreted as a downright insult when done in Canada.

In today's world, Body Language is a subset of Kinesics, which is the study of non-verbal communication. This has quickly become an integral part of societal living in today's world because if you do not know how to make your body work for you as a sigma male, you will end up with a lot of casualties, enemies, and misinterpretations of your hands.

The assignment of this chapter is to show you how to move your body the way you want it to. By the end of this chapter, you should know the movements and body language that is befitting for successful sigma males - the one you are quickly evolving to be.

Why Is Body Language Important?

You are probably asking. "What's the fuss about how I carry my body and how I use it when I am trying to communicate with people or when I am in a public setting?"

Well, here are the reasons for which body language is vital.

1. In social contexts, people do not just listen out for the things you say with your mouth alone. They also try to pay attention to your body so that they can understand what's truly going on in your mind every time. When you know this and understand how to control your body language, you can ensure that your mouth and overall body energy say the same thing. This sets you up for massive opportunities in every regard.

2. Body language is one skill that comes closest to mind reading. If you have done your best to develop psychic abilities to no avail, having a clear grasp of body language will help you out here. It can help you make informed financial/business decisions, move out of danger when you are faced with it, and also positions you to tell a lot about the person you are trying to read.

3. Non-verbal communication is better and more important than words. Everyone can say anything. However, when someone isn't comfortable with something, his body language toward you changes for some reason. When you

have mastered the art of not speaking against them, you can analyze their moves and predictably tell what they are trying to do, plus how they must make it work.

The Posture of a Sigma Male

This is one part of the message where everything comes to play. To get the most out of the people you interact with, you must know that you are a king and commit to carrying yourself as one. As already stated, your posture says a lot about you. It tells a lot about your confidence, competence, and even the way you see the people you interact with on a daily basis.

Here's how to posture like the important and high-flying man you are.

About Your Choice of Clothes

1. The statement "You are addressed the way you dress" has never been truer than it is in today's world. If you are still of the mindset that books shouldn't be judged by their covers, you are right. The only challenge is that you are not a book.
2. As a rule of thumb, dress like you have somewhere more important to be later. This way, you eliminate the chances that you would show up to a place underdressed. Nevertheless, the best fashion tip we can give you at this time is to strive to understand the context. Let the occasion determine your choice of what to wear.

3. In a later chapter, we will get into more details about the fashion aspect of things. Keep your ears and eyes open.

About Your Gait

1. The first guide to good posture is to understand what good posture actually means for a man. First of all, good posture means that your ears, shoulders, waist, and knees should all align in a straight line.

   To make this more memorable, imagine there's an imaginary pole connecting all these parts of your body together. Keep this in mind the next time you are about to walk out of your house.

2. Start with posture exercises. These exercises help to strengthen your core muscles so that you do not walk like you just stepped out of a winepress. There are easy ones you can try out at home, and all you need is a little patience and just a few clicks of some buttons on YouTube.

   This is the first step to having the posture of a winning sigma male. You have to exercise and prep your body to always be alert.

3. In addition to doing those reps, focus on controlling what you eat. Cut out excess carbs and junk from your overall meal. In addition to predisposing you to health conditions relating to excess cholesterol in the body, these foods make you put on

unnecessary weight and actually force you out of shape earlier than you may have thought.

4. A quick tip to help you understand what good posture you should have is to stand flush against a wall. Let your back, the back of your head, and your butt rest against the wall. Keep this picture in mind for the next time you are about to stand up and walk.

5. While standing, your chin should be parallel to the floor, not inclined toward the floor or pointing upwards.

6. When you take a quick look at yourself in the mirror, your body should have that aligned look. This means that your shoulders must be at the same height, and both sides of your hip bones must be aligned as well.

7. Walk with long, confident steps. The way you walk says a lot about you. When you walk with long and confident steps, you give off the vibe of being the man in charge who has the luxury of walking like he owns the place. This can instantly set you up for massive opportunities (especially in social gatherings) as it makes people believe that you have all it takes to be a self-sufficient man.

8. Greet people with a confident smile on your face and a twinkle in your eyes. Let your voice communicate warmth when you speak to them. A good way to get the hang of this is to start trying it out with the people in your life (the people you are already comfortable around). Ask them to rate you

and provide any cues they think may help you achieve the overall look of a relaxed and in-charge man who is meeting someone else for the first time.

9. When you are introduced to a person for the first time, and you are about to go for a handshake, remember that there are rules to doing that the right way. For one, go for a firm handshake. The web between your thumb and index fingers should connect with theirs. Look them in the eyes while you go for that handshake and introduce yourself with a smile on your face.

   However, do not press their hands as it can come off as a rude way of interacting with people, especially strangers.

10. Unless it is absolutely necessary, do not sit down for long. This is because it is infinitely more difficult to keep good posture in place when sitting than when standing. However, if it is impossible to avoid sitting for long (maybe due to the nature of the job you do), you may want to start by getting yourself ergonomic chairs and tables. These provide some level of comfort and can easily be manipulated to suit your unique needs.

11. When walking, try to pull your stomach in. This gives your body an asymmetrical look and also greatly improves the general look of your physique. This is especially helpful when you are on the prowl for a romantic interest as it increases

the chances that the people you have noticed would be attracted to you as well.

12. Allow your hands to hang naturally by your sides when you stand. One easy way to know if your shoulders are in the right position is to look at the alignment of your hands at the sides of your torso. If the back of your palms points forward, it's a sign that something is wrong with your posture. When your shoulders are in the right position, your thumbs will be pointing forward while your palms point toward your body.
13. Standing? Remember to keep your feet shoulder-width apart and place the bulk of your weight on the balls (or soles) of your feet. When you are in the right position, it wouldn't be quite easy to topple you over, even when you aren't readily braced for impact.

How to Communicate Dominance, Ooze Power, and Radiate Charm When the Needs Arise Without Speaking

Try these out.

1. One of the first ways to ooze charm and personality every single time is to wear a broad smile on your face. A smile makes you look younger, more endearing, and also makes you seem more approachable. Extra brownie points for you if you have the perfect teeth - that's literally an asset right there.

2. Most of how you are perceived in social circles are influenced by the choice of clothes you wear. This is why you must invest in looking good (especially as a sigma male who has come to terms with the fact that he was made for more in his life). We'll get to fashion in another chapter of this book. However, keep in mind that you won't escape what you decide to wear.
3. Greet people with a firm handshake whenever you meet them for the first time. Ensure the handshake meets the criteria you were shown in the last section of this chapter. Another simple way to send across the subliminal message that you are in charge is to hold the person's hand for a few seconds longer than the handshake should have lasted while maintaining strong eye contact.
4. Size is almost always related to importance and dominance. This is why it is easier for men who are huge to be interpreted as being important almost immediately. If you haven't been blessed with a bulky physique, try making yourself look a bit bigger than you really are.

To accomplish this, avoid slouching when you walk into and around the room. Place your hands on your hips (when you can, like mid-conversation) as this makes your elbows go wider and can give the illusion that you are slightly bigger than you actually are. At the same time, slightly thrust your chest out as this also contributes to the size advantage you are looking for.

5. Establish dominance by being the tallest man in the room (or at least give off the vibes that you are the tallest man in the room). To accomplish this, start by wearing shoes that complement your height. They don't have to be high-heeled, but you can easily find shoes with soles that are a bit off-the-ground.

    Also, stand up straight when you walk.

6. Establish dominance by using the principle of ownership. This simply means that you have to find a way to communicate to everyone that you aren't the regular kind of guy by owning something that regular people only wish they could get in their lifetime.

    This could be things like a Rolex, a limited-edition car, or even some obvious designer clothes. Only go down this route if you have the means to afford whatever you want to brandish and if you think it is completely necessary. If you can't afford it or you don't believe it is necessary, you may want to try other points.

7. Assume dominant positions when you attend social gatherings. This could be sitting at the head of a table, walking down the center of an aisle with your confident gait, standing with your back to a group of people, and not being afraid that you may get attacked from behind.

The idea behind this is to pass across the message that you are the person who calls the shots under these conditions.

8. Take charge of time when you are in social gatherings. Some subtle ways to do this is by finding the most diplomatic ways to keep the conversation centered around you when you converse with people, taking an early exit from an event (which gives the vibe that you have other equally or more important things to catch up with), or arriving 'fashionably late.'

   Again, these tips can easily make you be considered as being arrogant. So, it is up to you to decide the best-case scenarios where you get to use them. When you are in the midst of your superiors, it may not be a good idea to use these.

9. Let your face tell the same story. One simple way to note the dominant man in any group is to take a look at the faces of the people represented there. When you see the dominant man, you'd easily tell because his face tells it all.

   He can easily swap from wearing an approving smile to pulling off an annoyed snarl or just putting on a disappointed, blank stare when the needs arise. In any case, train your face to be as expressive as it should be.

10. At some point, you'd soon meet with other people who would want to play the dominance game on you. They'd do all they

could to make you wilt into your shell. Well, it is up to you to make sure that this doesn't happen to you.

When you meet these people, here are a few things to try out.

- You'd know them from the firmness of their handshake. Match their intensity, and be sure you lock your gaze with theirs.
- Find a way to touch them before they get the chance to touch you. This could be by playfully placing a full palm on their shoulder mid-joke or just brushing your palm down the sleeve of their tux while 'admiring the material.'
- They would try to cut you out when you speak. Negate this by speaking a bit louder, faster, or by simply telling them to stand down and "let me finish."

How to Read Anyone Like an Open Book - The Skill of Expert Interpretation of Body Language

Now that we have critically examined how to make body language work for you (especially in corporate settings and social gatherings), it is time to take a look at how you can use this skill of expert body language reading to decode what a person is feeling at every time.

The good thing about this is that if you learn how to do it well, you will always be ahead of every other person in your life. You can tell a person's next actions and come up with a plan or counterplan to make sure their actions end up with you getting whatever you want out of them.

Understanding body language is important in every ramification, from the corporate setting to your relationships/romance and even the quality of your friendships.

Without further ado, here's how to interpret body language and also some tips to help you get started. Consider these general rules, and people tend to pass these messages across subliminally.

Raised Eyebrows Generally Signify Discomfort

The next time you are in a conversation with someone, and they suddenly raise their eyebrows at you, it could be that they are uncomfortable about something you have said or done. Then again, it could also be that they don't quite believe a statement you have made, or they think of it as impossible.

A raised eyebrow could mean discomfort or disbelief.

Crossed Arms Usually Suggest That They Don't Accept Your Ideas

People become confrontational when they are faced with ideas that do not sit well with them. It is just a normal thing to see a person get all defensive when you present new ideas that go against all they have held onto for their entire lives.

When you are talking to someone, and their arms are folded, you may want to rethink your entire strategy because it could be that all you are saying is falling on deaf ears.

Mirroring is a Good Thing

Mirroring is simply the act of copying someone else's body language. Many times, humans tend to do it subconsciously as we do not give a lot of thought to the action.

Usually, mirroring only happens when someone feels a strong connection with you or they resonate completely with the conversation at hand. So, does it feel like the person sitting opposite you is mimicking all your moves (or most of them)? Take that as a good sign and focus on making the conversation more memorable than it already is.

Nodding Too Much? They May Feel Spooked

A nod is a sign that someone agrees with something you have said or done. However, when it feels too much and too rushed, it could also mean something else; that they feel spooked and trapped in one corner. When you are talking to someone, and it seems like they just can't stop nodding, it could be that they are worried about what you think about them and would do anything to ensure you keep having a good impression of them.

So, nodding is good. Too much nodding? Not too good!

Look Deeply into the Eyes

The eyes are the windows to the soul, right? This doesn't only mean that a person's soul interacts with the world through their eyes. It also means that you can look deeply into their eyes and have an idea of what they are thinking or feeling at any time.

When someone is lying to you, it may be difficult for them to hold steady eye contact. Also, someone who stares too deeply into your eyes when talking could be using this to cover up the fact that something they are saying isn't entirely true. This one is a double-edged sword.

Again, if someone cannot seem to meet your eyes when you are talking to them, it could signify submissiveness, bashfulness, or timidity. It could also be a sign of a guilty conscience. At the end of the day, it is up to you to determine the one that most applies to the specific situation at hand.

How Close Are They Standing?

Proximity is also another cue to look out for. When someone views you in a good light and wants to be associated with you, they tend to stand or sit closer to you. When they are scared of you or think of you as someone they wouldn't want to be associated with, they would rather stay worlds away from you, even if they have to sit across a table.

On the other hand, if they unconsciously back away when you come closer or flinch when you try to reach out to them, that could be a sign that they don't want you up in their personal spaces. It is now up to you to figure out why.

Keep Your Eyes on Their Feet

Not many people know the power of feet in nonverbal communication, and this is what makes the feet a great asset for you. When someone feels comfortable and into whatever you are talking to them about (when both of you are in a conversation), there's every possibility that their feet would be pointing toward you. When they have somewhere else they would rather be, you would notice that their feet may be pointing toward the door.

On the other hand, people also seem to communicate pressure and stress by incessantly tapping their feet on the ground. Tapping feet could also be a sign that someone is trying to suppress anger.

What Does a Real Smile Look Like?

It is important to tell the difference between a real and fake smile almost immediately. This keeps you on the same page with whoever you are conversing with. A real smile touches every part of the face and doesn't just stop with the mouth alone.

When a person genuinely smiles, their eyes light up. The sides of their eyes crinkle, and their mouths may crack open. The only way to tell if a smile is genuine or not is to look into the eyes of the person smiling and also listen out for the sound of their laughter (if they are laughing). Real laughter wouldn't sound forced to you.

Bringing It All Together

Imagine the power you would wield when you step into a room, and you can basically tell what the next person is thinking simply by reading their body like a book.

Even if you don't consider yourself to be psychic, you can tell a lot about what a person is thinking every time simply by carefully observing their bodies and how they respond to the people around them. You can use the pieces of information you gather to determine whether or not they accept whatever you are saying.

Again, when you can tell what a person thinks about you from how they act around you, you can decide how to navigate your relationship with them. You can now tell if you should spend more time trying to get them to be comfortable around you or if it is the perfect time for you to make any moves you may want to make.

This is also an important way to advance your life and career because, for one, you can easily tell if your boss likes you or not with what his body language tells you when you hang out with him. Use the information gathered to determine the next course of action as you climb your way up the corporate or business ladder.

The next chapter of this book will cover a salient conversation every sigma male must have with himself; sooner or later.

Chapter Summary

1. Body language is a part of nonverbal communication that can shed so much light on what a person feels every time. If you understand body language and how to read people like a book, you have an advantage over them because you can easily use the information you get from them to prepare your winning strategy in every scenario.
2. Understanding body language is not as difficult as you think. It all starts with paying keen attention the next time you are hanging out with someone. Look out for how they respond to you and the environment at large. Then again, you become

better with body language as you consciously spend more time reading people's body language.

Chapter 6: The Sigma Male and Fashion

You've read it many times in this book already. "Dress the way you want to be addressed."

Well, this is the chapter where we will get to unpack that statement and make it make sense to you.

Fashion is an integral part of the life of every successful sigma male. The man who knows that he is headed for the pinnacle of his life understands that he doesn't have the luxury of looking anything less than exquisite, and you will see him putting his best foot forward every single time he has to make decisions about what to wear, how to wear it, and when to wear it.

Your fashion sense makes a subliminal statement about you. Just like your body language, what you wear says a lot more about you than almost any other thing. Then again, people first see you before they hear you, and you know what they say about how important first impressions are, right?

Then again, another reason why you must pay attention to the way you dress is simply because of influence. Whether you know it or not, your life influences someone, somewhere, who would give anything to be like you. This is even truer for you if you have sons, younger men in your life that you play guardian to (people like smaller cousins or nephews), or if you hang around men a lot. Even if they do not come and tell you this, there are so many men who look up to you, and your fashion choices inspire the way they eventually dress.

Take a quick look at all the sigma men in your life. Can you even begin to imagine how their fashion choices have come together to make you the man you are today (in terms of the looks you mostly wear)? You may be surprised to know that the hairstyle you are wearing now was influenced by your favorite TV star, while your default choice of sneakers became the obvious choice after you saw your best male author rocking them to one of his book signing events.

If they had these effects on you, do you not think that your own fashion choices will affect the men in your life as well? Even if you do not think it is important to dress up well, think about all the men who are looking up to you and commit to doing a good job, even if it is for their sake.

Now that we have that settled, let's help you make sense of your fashion sense as well.

Understanding Trends, Knowing Your Body Type, and Discovering the Power of Comfortable and Simplistic Fashion

"Fashion is pain."

If you are a fashion freak, you have probably heard that statement before. Most designers use it as a way to explain some of the most alarming things you would see as you journey through vast fashion galleries. When you walk through these galleries and see clothes that have been made from the most uncomfortable fabrics, or you see plus sized men who have been folded into clothes that are at least 2 sizes smaller than their body size, you may be left to ask yourself what the essence of everything is.

Then again, when you see these men hunched inward, unable to breathe properly, or tucked away into skinny jeans that feel itchy against the inner parts of their thighs/balls, you may be tempted to actually believe that fashion and comfort do not go hand in glove.

Well, this isn't entirely true.

Aside from their obvious reason (which is to cover our nakedness), clothes are worn for comfort. Protecting you from the harsh elements of nature means that they should be able to provide comfort for you as well. It makes no sense that you get dressed up in clothes that keep you uncomfortable and prevent you from living your life to the fullest simply because you decided to dress up in them. So, the first thing you want to ensure before you select any outfit as a sigma male is that they are the perfect fit for you and your body is comfortable inside the clothes you have selected.

If you get dressed in any outfit and feel the slightest hint of discomfort, that could be a sign that you may want to try putting on something else.

This is why it is important that you understand your body size and the style that works best for you. This way, you can make informed choices, and you can find an effective way to blend your love for style with comfort as well. None should be sacrificed for the other.

The next thing you must consider when it comes to your fashion style is trendiness. There's no way to shy away from the conversation that trends play a serious role in fashion and what is considered to be acceptable per time. Since the early 1900s, trends have played a significant role in how people dress. From the days of trousers with larger-sized legs and suspenders until these days that are characterized by trendier styles, understanding what is acceptable and even considered to be a trend in your world can give you a leg up when you are selecting your outfit for the next social event you have to attend.

In essence, while selecting the perfect outfit for your needs, here are some things you must consider.

Your Personal Preferences

While it is possible to be influenced by the fashion choices of others, there's no rule that says you must mirror another person to the teeth. Remember that as a sigma male, one of the traits you must protect with everything you have is your uniqueness.

The first step to making the most out of your outfits is to start by defining your style. Are you a "jeans and t-shirt" kind of guy? Do you love the feeling that comes from dressing down and adding a bowtie at the same time? Whatever feels like you should take center stage when you set up your wardrobe.

Yes, you would eventually get other clothes, but it's best to have more of what you actually like in your closet. Not sure of what to still get? We will make some suggestions in the next section of this chapter.

Comfort

Nothing is worse than having to spend hours in an outfit that is anything but comfortable. Comfort (when it comes to fashion and picking out the right clothes) is also mostly dependent on the size of what you have picked out. This is why it is important that you always deal with designers that are worth their salt. This way, even if you aren't sure of your exact sizes/dimensions, they can always make recommendations or help you out.

Your Body Structure

Your posture says a lot about you. In addition to that, it also determines the kind of clothes you can get away with wearing and those that you may pay heavily for even attempting to put on.

Here's a clear case-in-point scenario. If you have drooping shoulders, it won't make much sense for you to try wearing t-shirts that are too tight on your body. This is because a combination of those 2 (drooping shoulders and tight t-shirts) may not give a very pleasant image to the eyes. Instead, you may want to consider wearing double-breasted suits since they come with shoulder pads that can contribute to giving your overall upper body posture that asymmetrical look it needs to stand out in social gatherings.

When you have considered these 3 factors together, you should be able to come up with an outfit that is the perfect choice for every single event you have to attend. Then again, dressing up wouldn't be a harrowing experience for you.

Into the Wardrobe of a True Sigma Male

If you want to be addressed as a true sigma male, you've got to nail the dress code down to a 'T.' How do you accomplish this if you do not even know what the wardrobe and clothing choices of high-performing sigma males look like?

Well, here's some much-needed help in this section of the book.

Start with a Little Variety

When you step into the closet of a true sigma male, one of the things you would easily notice is his ability to have a little bit of everything. Any kind of clothing you look for would probably be there. This includes tuxedos, plain clothes, chinos, jeans, and everything you can think of. In the shoe department, you are probably going to see a mix of loafers, corporate shoes, and even trainers.

Do you know why the sigma male does this?

It is because he understands how volatile life can be. He can be called upon at any time to lead a delegation and would be required to be dreaded down with a suit and tie to go with it. Or, he can get an invite to a casual party and wouldn't have all the time in the world to take a quick detour into the closest clothes store.

Stick with Solid Colors

Okay. If this sounds a bit far-fetched to you (because you are the type of man who loves his clothes bright-colored), you may want to scratch that. However, regardless of what you do, ensure that you have the requisite amount of solid-colored clothes in your wardrobe - especially if you have a corporate job.

Colors like black, white, navy blue and grey should be abundant in your closet. This way, you do not have to always worry that you do not have the clothes needed when you have to make a formal appearance or presentation. Then again, these colors can almost never go wrong. So, why pass out on the opportunity of stashing your closet full of colors that are easy-to-be-combined?

Sweatshirts and Drawstring Pants

You know summer is fast approaching, right? Bear this in mind when you walk into the nearest clothes store to change out your wardrobe.

Some of the essential wardrobe supplies you should have as sigma males are sweatshirts and drawstring pants. In addition to being extremely cozy and easy to just slip into, they offer you the privilege of wearing this "I just rolled out of bed looking this hot" look. They also serve as the best outfit when you want to show up for a less-than-formal event.

For the best results, ensure you get a grey, black, and white sweatshirt and pants. Any other colors you choose to get are up to you.

A Carefully-Selected Stash of Well-Fitting or Slightly-Larger T-Shirts

Even the most serious sigma males all get to the point where they get out of their suits and just carefully shrug into their t-shirts. For one, t-shirts are indescribably cozy. Then again, most of them are made from cotton, making them the best material for comfort as they are easy to wash, easy on the skin, and able to absorb sweat (if you are the type who sweats a lot).

Then again, you can just combine the right t-shirt with just about anything. You can pull it off with a nice pair of suits, or you may combine it with your favorite jeans for a dapper look. If you are feeling adventurous, you can even try wearing collared t-shirts tucked into a pair of plain trousers with a powerful pair of loafers to finish off this look.

Can't you already imagine how ridiculously handsome you would look in this outfit?

Solid-Colored Suits

Because why not?

As a sigma male, you can't swap suits for anything else in your closet. If you would be attending corporate events or you have intentions of making a powerful first impression on people, there's no running away from suits.

Suits are a precarious situation, though. If you haven't yet mastered the art of selecting the perfect suit for your body style and frame, you may be frustrated when you end up with coats that hang off your body frame. So, it is best you work with a designer when you make your pick of suits.

Also, ensure you have black, navy blue, and grey-colored suits for starters. Any other colors you choose to get are up to you.

Roll Neck Shirts

Roll Neck shirts have a way of making you look like an undercover FBI agent. They give you that smoking hot look and, if worn well, can increase your chances of landing your dream date the next time you attend a party. The good thing about roll-neck shirts is that you can make them look anyhow you want them to.

You can wear them in a corporate way or make them fit the casual wear frame easily. Then again, extra brownie points for you if you have a muscular frame. Roll Neck shirts will look extremely good on you.

At Least One Designer's Wristwatch

One thing people look at once they meet you (especially in social and corporate gatherings) is your wrist. A way to inspire the admiration of the people around you is by knowing the right kind of wristwatch to wear and then actually wearing it. Get yourself at least one designer wristwatch (if you can afford it) and watch what happens to you the next time you attend a formal event.

Dress Shoes

Dress shoes are a must-have for high-performing sigma males. There are times when the best trainers in the market wouldn't cut it, and you would need to wear corporate or dress shoes. You need to get the perfect fit before that time comes.

A Pair of Sandals

Many men do not think of these as important, but sandals can be a lifesaver for you. If you are gunning for a casual look, sandals may just be a perfect choice. Then again, is there any better way to show off your perfectly-sculpted toes than to put on a pair of sandals?

Trainers

If you're into them, you should consider getting yourself a few pairs. Trainers always save the day. Then again, they are perfect for casual outfits like jeans and whatever you choose to wear the jeans with, chinos, or even when you are rocking a pair of drawstring pants and a sweatshirt.

Personal Effects

This simply speaks of the personal items in your closet that make you 'you.' Your cologne, body spray, deodorants, and every other thing that contributes to giving you that divine body scent you wish to rock all day long.

When you find the product that does it for you, please stick with it and make sure you use it. Remember, the power of your unique scent cannot be overemphasized.

How to Understand Your Sense of Style and Radiate Confident Superiority as a Sigma Male

In addition to having a closet that is up to par, you must understand how to own your sense of style so that you can look like the guy who is confident in what he puts on his body. Here are the steps to follow to better understand your sense of style and ooze that dominance you need for the next stage of your life.

Look at Fashion Inspirations

This doesn't mean you have to turn into a fashion vixen. It simply just means that you may want to consider spending more time seeing and not just looking. Take some time to look at your friends, coworkers, and family members whose styles you like. Can you find the parallels in their fashion statements? What are the specific things about their fashion sense that you like?

Look at Your Own Closet

We already talked about how one of the first things you must consider when it comes to fashion is how comfortable it makes you. This is why you have to look at yourself first.

While trying to figure out the fashion accessories you like, do not forget to look at what you have a lot of at the moment. If you have much of it right now, the chances are that this is the case because you like it.

Use Mood Boards

This is simply where you congregate all your inspiration ideas together. Think of a mood board as a fashion dump. When you find a style you love and would love to replicate, get it and place it on your mood board. If it is from the pages of a book or magazine, you can cut it out and stick it on this board. If you stumbled across the image online, you can easily download it and save it to your mood board folder.

At intervals, take a deep breath and study all the pieces on this mood board. No matter how disjointed these photos seem to be, you will find some parallels if you look long and hard enough.

Try Unique Style Choices

You wouldn't know if you truly like a thing until you try it out, right? This is the same case with your sense of style. From time to time, step out of your comfort zone and try out new fashion styles. You may just find something that resonates with you, something you least expected.

Making a Fashion Statement

This is also another thing you want to pay attention to as a sigma male. If you do not master the art of making a fashion statement, you may end up lost in the crowd every single time you step out for events or go for public functions.

Your fashion statement is what makes your choice of clothes unique and memorable. If your statement is loud enough, you may be surprised at the rate at which people would want to flock toward you and do your bidding. There are a few tips to help you make a fashion statement immediately.

Wear Sunshades Every Time You Can

There's just something about sunshades that gives you the "James Bond" look, and you would need this James Bond look for everything, especially to get the attention of your love interest.

Combine the James Bond Look with Insane Clothing Choices

We have already started talking about how to select the best outfits for your needs and also some of the best combination choices for you. This is the time to get down and dirty, then decide the best kind of clothes that suit your needs.

When you have nailed the sunshades look to a 'T,' and you combine it with the perfect outfit, you are already well on your way to making a loud-enough fashion statement.

Your Hairstyle is Key

This wouldn't take a lot of time because the golden idea here (if you are still unsure of the perfect hairstyle) is to visit a competent hairstylist and ask them to work their magic on you. They would consider the shape of your face, the shape of your skull, and any obvious imperfections they have to cover up before deciding on the perfect hairstyle for you.

This should be a part of the general mix as you prepare to make a loud fashion statement.

Finish Off with the Perfect Accessories, Choice of Scents, and Shoes

This should be the final thing you think about as you prepare to step out in style. Your accessories must be on point. You should have invested some cool cash into getting a nice-enough wristwatch by now. Again, if you are still single, you may want to consider keeping your fingers free of rings or just wearing a minimal number of rings (1 at most). This is because having too many rings at the same time gives off an unserious vibe. In the same vein, you may want to consider keeping your wrists bare of unneeded bangles. These especially apply when you are attending corporate events and functions.

When you are done, think about the shoes you want to wear and the scent you must pull off to complete the look you are rocking. This is how to make a fashion statement every single time you want to go out.

Lastly, Understand the Principle of Being Fashionably Late

First of all, what does it mean to be fashionably late?

Simply put, the concept of being fashionably late means to arrive behind time at an event that doesn't necessarily require that you be extraneously punctual. This concept started becoming more generally accepted with the rise of recent media platforms. You see your best stars doing it, where they swagger into an event and captivate an audience with how dramatic their entry can be. As far as an otherwise quiet congregation is concerned, anything as dramatic as the knock of the soles of your shoes against the ground can be a cause for all eyes to turn to you.

If you aren't shy of being at the receiving end of attention (which you shouldn't be), being fashionably late should be the last nail in the 'style' coffin.

However, it is important to note that this isn't appropriate under every condition. There are times that not being punctual can strip you of massive opportunities. It is entirely up to you to know when to go this route and when to impress people with your skills of punctuality.

Chapter Summary

1. As a sigma male, you do not have the luxury of leaving your looks to chance. This is because you are addressed with the way you choose to dress.
2. This entire chapter has been dedicated to helping you understand your sense of style, choose the perfect outfits for all your events, and make a fashion statement every single time you have to step out of your house. Use the strategies discussed in this chapter to improve your overall looks.

You'll be surprised at the new opportunities that will start coming your way when you become intentional about owning the narrative of your fashion.

Chapter 7: The Principle of Self-Multiplication

How to Win Over Friends, Acquire Allies, and Influence People Even Without Being a Positional Leader

If you are asked right now to make a simple list of all the leaders around you, you'd most likely make a long list of people and may never think to add yourself to that list.

This is because, as far as you are concerned, you aren't a leader because you aren't heading a department at work or because you aren't the parents or 1st child at home.

While these people you may have mentioned are recognized leaders, one thing you must learn is that leadership is more about the person and their mindset than it is about the position they occupy. The people you are looking up to (bosses at work, politicians of this world, your parents/guardians) are all positional leaders. They are considered leaders by virtue of the positions they occupy. While this is a valid classification of leadership, it isn't the only leadership classification because any responsible man is a leader.

Then again, you don't have to wait until you become that person before you resume leadership activities and take responsibility.

In this chapter, we will show you how to wield insane influence over the people in your world, even if you are not "the recognized leader' of the group. This will be brief and practical.

The Concept of Influence and Why You Need It as a Sigma Male

One of the most-used words in today's world is influence. This is because of the power this word carried. Influence is simply your ability to have an effect on the character, development, choices, and behavior of the people around you.

With this in perspective, you need to be influential because of a number of cardinal reasons. Here are some of them.

1. Influence makes you likable. When people like you, they would be more inclined toward helping you achieve your goals. Then again, this can make all the difference in your life and career.
2. Influence allows you to strike an emotional connection with people. When this connection is in place, it is easier to reach out to them and have a real impact on their lives. The easiest way to make a tangible change in the life of a person is by connecting with them emotionally.
3. When you are influential, it reduces the number of people who would want to come against you. People would know that you aren't just to be trifled with and would rather stay away from contending with you. This can also come in handy as you make your way to the top.
4. Then again, the influential one is the visible one. The visible one is the first to get all the goodies when they come knocking.

How the Sigma Male Starts and Maintains Platonic Relationships

One of the main questions people have asked over time is how the sigma male is able to start, grow, and maintain platonic relationships like a boss. The way he is respected by the people in his world and is blessed with people who would go all out for him is an enigma to many.

As a sigma male, here's how to start and maintain platonic relationships so that they grow and bless you with all the benefits that can come from having healthy platonic relationships.

Be the Kind of Man People Want to Associate With

The first step to making your platonic friendships work is by being the kind of man that people want to be associated with, the goal-oriented man who has his sights set on where he is headed in life and who would stop at nothing to have his friends win with him.

Then again, your values must be clear to you. It is almost impossible to have deep and meaningful relationships with people who don't share similar values.

Establish and Reinforce Boundaries

This is most important when you are trying to build a platonic friendship with someone who you wouldn't mind being in a romantic relationship with. It is important to remind yourself that what you are up to is a platonic relationship and not a romantic one. This would help you keep yourself and your feelings in check.

Be Committed to Them

Nothing strengthens a friendship better than when the other person can tell that you are genuinely invested in their growth and development. When you can prove that you are committed to them and they return the gesture, you are already on your way to having a relationship that will stand the test of time.

Communicate

Communication isn't only needed in romantic relationships but in platonic friendships too. If two humans commit to themselves (even on a platonic level), they must be willing and ready to communicate like emotionally-mature adults. Have deep conversations and let them know that you are bringing them into your life.

This places value on them and also allows them to do the same for you.

Be the First to Invest in the Relationship

To make your platonic relationships work, do not be that person who is always on the receiving end or begging for something. Invest in the relationship as well. Let the other person look at you and wonder why you would go all out for them and the relationship.

Investing in a relationship of this nature will also get the other person to want to commit as much time, energy, and resources as you have committed (if they are sane), and this helps you build a strong relationship.

Make Space for Their Flaws

The best way to stay sane is to remind yourself that the best person you will meet is still a human being and will eventually make mistakes. This way, forgiving them and finding common grounds to move on wouldn't be difficult.

Know When to Cut Your Losses and Prioritize Your Mental Health

The goal is to build a platonic relationship that is healthy and empowers you, not to open your life up to leeches and parasites that will suck you dry and leave you to die.

Then again, ensure that you have a strong process for qualifying the people who you seek to invest this much time and energy into building strong relationships with. The truth is that not everyone is worth it in the end.

How to Make Other Dominant Men Like and Respect You By Using Likability and Influence Strategies

It is one thing to meet men who would rather stay in the background and be happy with being the nameless face. What if you meet dominant men who expect to be respected, feared, and even venerated in a group? How do you interact with them in such a way that they respect you, give you the credit that is due to you, and still feel like they aren't being threatened while you ascend to the heights you want to get?

Here are a few ways to achieve that.

Be Exceptionally Good at Your Craft

No matter how domineering a man is, he cannot resist the allure of having a gifted and excellent man in his sphere. In fact, the more gifted you are, the more the chances that dominant men would want to keep you closer to them and treat you like their equals.

Use the Strategies Documented in Chapter 5

Many dominant men would want to be sure that you are fit to be in their world. This is why they would test you first and watch how you respond to their domineering moves first. If they interpret you to be anything short of strong-willed, they may not respect you.

Chapter 5 documented many strategies that aimed at showing you how to let the dominant man know that you aren't to be trifled with as well. Use all those strategies to your good.

Be a Man of Your Word

If the dominant male perceives that you aren't to be trusted, he instantly loses any ounce of respect he may have had for you. Prevent this by sticking to your word every single time.

As far as this scenario is concerned, it is much better to refrain from giving your word than to find yourself having to rescind your promises every other time.

Look Respectable

The dominant alpha male sizes you up before anything else. If he thinks that you don't look the part, he may never take you seriously. So, start by looking at the part. A previous chapter went into detail on the fashion aspect of things. Revisit that chapter if need be.

Chapter Summary

1. Self-multiplication is all about understanding that influence is a game you must play and be intentional about winning.
2. This chapter has focused on showing you how to build strong platonic friendships with other go-getters. Use the strategies discussed in this chapter to harness these relationships and also get the dominant, alpha men around you to respect you.
3. Note that alpha men may not come around immediately because of their reputation. However, stick to playing the long-term game, and they will come to respect you over time.

Chapter 8: The Sigma Male and His Romantic Conquests

Romance is an important part of every man's life. Most men seek to meet the love of their lives, fall for them, probably settle down, and build the life of their dreams with them. If you have had these dreams, do not beat yourself up because you are not alone.

However, you must understand that a sigma male starts and supports his romantic relationships in ways that may be considered unconventional. Anyways, this chapter will show you how to go about your love relationships as a winning sigma male.

Boxes to Tick Off Before Looking for a Significant Other as a Sigma Male

Before you even start looking to commit to a relationship as a sigma male, here are some of the things you should get off your to-do list.

Your Values

If you still don't know what your values are, you may have a hard time in relationships because you may end up dating people who have beliefs that are completely different from yours.

Independence

One of the worst enemies of successful relationships is dependence. As a sigma male, you must have a mind of your own before seeking a relationship. In fact, it is also important that you have a space of your own, especially if you are looking for a relationship that will eventually lead to marriage.

Financial Stability

Are you able to pay your bills comfortably? Do you make enough money that keeps you comfortable? If you answered these questions in the negative, you might want to consider holding off a bit.

Emotional Maturity

How well are you able to master your emotions and feelings? Do you even know your temperaments, and have you created a self-management plan for these temperaments?

If you haven't, you may want to do these first.

Knowing What You Want

What exactly do you want in a partner? How realistic are your desires? It is one thing to know what you want and another thing to want the things that are realistic. Take some time to evaluate the feasibility of your desires before committing yourself to any type of romantic relationship.

Understanding Ladies: How to Approach and Flirt with Them

Imagine you walk into a room full of people, and for some reason, your eyes are drawn to the lovely image of a lady (or person) seated in one corner of the room, and you feel a rush of emotions racing through your spine.

They look like someone you would want to pursue. However, the challenge right now is that there's so much space between both of you. More than anything else, you want to stand up, walk over to them, introduce yourself, and have a magical night (or even a magical life) with them.

Well, here's how to approach a lady (or your romantic love interest), start up a conversation with them, and hopefully get things going in the right direction.

Be Sure She is Interested in You

The first step to getting the attention of a lady is by getting out of that chair and making the first move. Try walking past her line of sight and making eye contact with her first. Does she track your movement with her eyes? Again, you would need the lessons from the chapter where we discussed body language to know for sure.

Look at her face. If you notice the slightest hint of a smile or it seems like she suddenly leans in your direction, it could be a sign that you should take the bull by the horn and start a conversation with her.

You Can Ask for Help

If there's a link somewhere (maybe, a mutual friend), you can ask them to introduce both of you. This way, you can skip the stairs and cut down on the initial awkwardness you may have battled with.

When You Get Her Attention

Getting a lady's attention is only the first step of the entire process. What you do with that attention is as important as getting the attention in the first place. This is where many guys get it wrong. They get one leg in the door and spend an inordinate amount of time talking about themselves like they are the next best thing to Clark Kent.

Believe me; you don't want to do that. Instead, here are a few things to try out:

- **Show genuine interest in her:** Ask about the things that matter to her, like what she does, what she studied, her hobbies, etc. The more interest you show, the more chances that she would be intrigued by you as well.
- **Make a genuine compliment:** This should even precede the conversation you would have with her. While exchanging pleasantries, take a good long look at her and spot out something that is worthy of being appreciated. Talk about that thing and appreciate her for it.
- **Hold eye contact and put a smile on your face:** As much as possible, try not to give a compliment that can easily be interpreted as 'obscene' or intrusive.
- **Allow her to set the pace of the conversation:** One thing you should know about your love interest is this. You aren't the only one scanning them. At the moment, you are also under their close watch, and you don't have the luxury of making even 1 mistake. So, be careful to make sure that she doesn't feel spooked in the conversation.

- **Let your sense of humor shine through:** Many ladies like a guy who can make them laugh. You can accomplish this by having a spot-on sense of humor. While flirting with a lady, you don't have to act all tough, high-strung, and unnecessarily macho. Let your guard down a bit and make her laugh. This is one way to get her to open up quickly.
- **Ask if she is seeing anyone at the moment:** You need to know if you should back off immediately or if it is safe to keep coming at her.

The Conversation Has Started, But...

The conversation should be well underway at this point. However, you need to show that you are a confident man. One way to do this is by ensuring that your physical posture remains the way it should be. Sit straight and ensure you hold eye contact. Let your smiles be bright and also have an effect on your eyes.

These are the subtle signs that let her know that you are confident in your skin as a man. Even if you are scared to death, doing these things will make her feel safe with you.

Find a Way to Touch Her

A light brush of skin can be the difference between a second date and the request to get her phone number that never turns out successfully. While flirting with a girl, touching is a powerful way to connect with her. This could be an innocent brush against her skin (if you are sitting side by side and you are close together), casually reaching out across the table to get something out of her (and then sliding the strand of hair into place behind her ear), or just getting a short hug from her at the end of the day.

In any case, pay close attention to ensure that your touches aren't intrusive or too much.

Watch Out for Other Signs

While having a nice time, watch out for other subtle signs. Does she hold your gaze as well? Does she laugh at your jokes? Can you see the faint signs of a blush on her cheeks? Does she feel flustered when your hands touch?

These may be signs that you are doing something right.

Ask for a Second Date

If you don't ask to meet again, she may not do so as well. So, to prevent the nagging pain you'd deal with afterward, when the time is coming to an end, carefully ask if she would like to meet up again.

If she accepts, you may go ahead to exchange contacts. This could be the start of a great love story.

The Attention Currency: How to Make a Girl Want You Without Oozing 'Predator' Vibes

Now that we have covered the subject of getting a girl's attention for the first time, here are a few things you can do to make the girl of your dreams want you as you want her without making her feel like you are stalking her.

Confidence Speaks Louder Than Words

Nothing speaks louder than the voice of confidence. And no, this doesn't mean that you have to strut around all day like an overbearing peacock. This means that you are just that guy who knows who he is, what he is worth, traits people with respect, and demands that the same should be done to him.

A Good Sense of Style

Ladies love suave men. If anything, they want to be able to show you off to their friends at public gatherings. They would love to pull their phones out on an evening out with the girls, show them your photo, and say, "oh, that's my man right there."

A Bit Off-Limits

One way to get a girl to want you and even start working her way towards you is by making her know that you are a bit off-limits. Usually, an effective way to do this is by whetting her appetite and then pulling back a bit.

So, when you have used the strategies covered in the last section of this chapter, and she has started getting invested in you, consider taking a few days off. During these days, just be a bit out of reach. When she is able to get back in touch, let her know that it wasn't anything she did wrong but the fact that you have had a lot to deal with. The aim of this activity is to pass that message across to her that although you love and cherish her, she also has her part to play in the relationship for it to be successful.

And that you wouldn't always be doing all the chasing as well.

Have a Good Reputation

Except for those who just like being with bad boys, most girls like to be with guys who have a good reputation. These guys are attentive and wouldn't consciously break their hearts. So, one way to make a girl want you is by being that guy who people can vouch for because you have been an honest man over time.

Have Your Own Life

When she knows that you have a ton of things to attend to and even many other ladies who would want to be with you, she would be more inclined toward letting you know that she is available for a relationship with you. This is important as it helps you build that connection quickly.

Sex and Building Long-Lasting Relationships

When it comes to relationships, there isn't any Holy Grail that details how your sex life should be. However, your personal beliefs should guide your decisions when it comes to sex. Also, both of you must be on the same page.

Are you abstaining from sex until you are married? Do you want to have sex with them now? How often should you have sex? These and more are the conversations you should have. Never assume that your partner wants sex without talking things over with them. This could cause a strain on the relationship when you find out that both of you are in the market for completely different things.

Then again, your sex life should be characterized by novelty. If you have the advantage of having your space to yourself, you may want to spice things up by trying out different locations and styles. In any case, the aim is to have fun and enjoy your partner.

Long-term relationships are built on the core values of

- Trust
- Loyalty
- Commitment
- Compromise, and
- Communication.

To have a long-term relationship that is healthy, all these elements must be in place. You must trust your partner fully, be loyal to them, commit to making the relationship work, be ready to compromise (while they do the same for you as well), and be open to heart-to-heart communication.

These are the only guarantees that your relationship as a Sigma Male will work.

Chapter Summary

1. The cheat sheet for sigma men's relationships is a bit different from that of other normal men. To have a successful and healthy relationship, you must know that you have to put in a lot of work to get your partner's attention and keep it.
2. Healthy relationships are formed on the values of trust, loyalty, commitment, compromise, and communication.

Chapter 9: Corporate and Career Dominance

Once you have figured many things out in your life, one of the next things you would have to figure out would be your career. As a sigma male, you most likely have visions of rising to the pinnacle of your career, sitting at the apex of what is possible to you, and making a lot of money at the same time.

Your dreams and aspirations are valid, dear sigma male. You just need to understand how to navigate life so that you get what you want.

In this chapter, we will walk you through some timeless principles of attaining corporate and career dominance.

How to Grow Your Career in Leaps and Bounds

Here are a few things you can start doing now to increase your chances of growing in your career within the shortest possible time. Most of your colleagues do not know these. Hence, they cannot apply these principles. So, applying them immediately will increase your chances of getting promoted as soon as possible.

Make Friends with the Boss

This is usually the first tip you should keep in mind if you intend to rise to the apex of your career within the shortest possible time. In a highly bureaucratic setting, your abilities may not be the only thing that is needed when there is a bigger opportunity on the ground. Under these circumstances, the most visible guy could be the one who gets the job.

So, from the first day you walk into that establishment, keep your ears to the ground and discover who the decision-makers are. Even on the board of decision-makers, there are key decision-makers. You want to have those guys on your side.

Do all you can to be friends with the boss. However, be loyal and do not snitch on your mates to get his favor. This could also be a test for him to know the type of person you are.

Be Openly Accountable

When others in your department are being shady, choose to be accountable. This will get you a couple of haters as people will say nasty things about you. However, it will get you accolades and open doors when the chips are down.

Even when your superiors do not ask you to, give detailed accounts of what you have done with the resources at your disposal and let them be the ones to judge you. Being the guy who is always accountable makes it easier to vest you with more responsibilities.

Ask the "How Can I Improve" Question

Once you have discovered who the decision-maker is, take one day to ask him how you can improve. This question can throw him off balance, but it also suggests that you will stop at nothing to see the organization get to the next level.

Again, it shows that you are a man of responsibility and who wouldn't love that kind of man getting more responsibilities at work?

Bring in Revenue

You do not have to be a part of the sales and marketing department to bring in revenue to the company. Whoever brings in sales and is consistent at that stands more chances of getting promoted whenever there's a window of opportunity.

You may start by thinking of how you can bring in clients to the company. Whenever you have figured this out, get to work on the ideas that come to you. At first, your bosses may behave like they don't see you. However, it is only a matter of time until they start thinking of rewarding you.

Study Those That Have Been Promoted Ahead of You

When you sit down to actually look at them, you will discover that regardless of what you think, there's a method to the madness. Whatever pattern you see them following, you may want to consider following it as well, as it increases the chances that you would get promoted too.

Never Shorten the Learning and Output Process

Even when you have risen to the apex of your career in that organization, do not be that man who becomes lousy about personal development. You would start deteriorating from the day you decide that it isn't important to keep learning and growing.

It's a given that producing more results is the only guarantee that you would be able to stay relevant, even at the top.

Dealing with a Difficult Boss and Navigating Treacherous Colleagues

Every worker's worst nightmare is having a difficult boss and being surrounded by treacherous colleagues. These two independent factors, when working together, can dramatically reduce your output at work.

In any case, if you have had the unlucky disadvantage of being blessed with both, here are some things you can do to get yourself out of this fix.

Make Up Your Mind on What You Want to Achieve

The first instrument an annoying boss will use against you is their obnoxiousness. They'll do all they can to frustrate you into giving them a good reason to sanction you. Do not give them this luxury.

From the start, decide that if you are going to be working under an annoying boss, you will give it your best shot, nonetheless. Ensure your mind is made up from the start, or you may not survive their annoyingness.

This also relates to your colleagues as well.

Never Discuss Your Boss with Coworkers

When you look at it, you never know who could be a snitch.

Take Responsibility When Necessary

Your boss is probably very good at nagging. One thing that would make them lose it even more is when something goes wrong, it is clearly your fault, and you try to make excuses for your actions or inactions. This makes them feel like you are trivializing the welfare of the organization.

Make Yourself Bully-Proof

A bad boss will only get to you when you allow them to. Making yourself bully-proof involves deciding that nothing your boss ever does will get under your skin. You will take instructions with a smile, handle criticism in good faith, and still carry out your responsibilities with all the dedication you have.

If you can do this, it is only a matter of time until they give up on trying to make your life a living hell.

If You Can, Ask to Be Transferred

If there's a boss above the boss that's bullying you (and you have access to them), you may want to consider the most diplomatic way to ask them to transfer you. If possible, let them make the transfer look anonymous. You can achieve this by writing them, sending a mail, or simply asking to see them.

As a rule of thumb, never complain to coworkers. They can't help you.

Talk to Your Boss

This applies when you are dealing with colleagues who are especially annoying. Never get confrontational with them. Instead, let your boss in on what's going on and allow a higher authority to mediate between all of you. This way, you allow them to handle the issue without complicating things for themselves.

Limit Your Interactions

This goes both ways, both for annoying colleagues and terrible bosses. At least, for the sanity of your mind, figure out the best way to interact less with them. Unless it is absolutely necessary, steer clear from their path.

Draw Strength from the Positives

It cannot be all bad. If it were, you would have quit a long time ago. This is the hard truth you may want to tell yourself. In that case, try channeling your energies to focus on the things that are good about your workplace.

This could be the money you are paid, the nice colleagues and friends you have met, and every other thing in-between. When you have something positive to hold on to, you give yourself the strength needed to deal with the negatives.

Know When to Quit

At some point, if the bullying goes on without any tangible changes, you may want to consider calling it quits. This could be a difficult one, and if you are going to go this route, ensure you spend quality time drafting your exit plan so that you aren't left high and dry with no income stream.

The Power of Decluttering

Sometimes, the reason you always have to deal with creative blocks at work isn't that you aren't good enough. It could just be for the single reason that you have a lot of clutter.

Now, this could be a literal or figurative statement.

As a literal statement, it could mean that you have a lot of unnecessary tidbits in your physical workspace, and you can benefit from having a little cleanup exercise. In that case, take a while to go through the things in your workspace and clear out everything that isn't necessary and doesn't aid your productivity. Burn those unnecessary notes. Let go of that device that keeps distracting you. Uninstall Social Media apps that just won't let you concentrate and give yourself the needed space to think creatively.

As a figurative statement, you may need to do more internal work. This could include letting go of limiting mindsets and things that have hurt you in the past, breaking out of nasty habits like procrastination, and just committing to being a better worker.

Then again, you would need to be in touch with your true self to make this work. This is why the last chapter will briefly touch on the subject of the sigma male and his sense of spirituality.

Chapter Summary

1. Career and corporate dominance are possible. You just know how to play the cards well so that you rise the corporate ladder as soon as possible.
2. Dealing with an annoying boss and petulant colleagues? The processes covered in this chapter can help you maintain your peace while you work your way out of this fix. Regardless of how overwhelming it may seem, there's always a way out of this challenge.

Chapter 10: The Sigma Male's Spirituality

If you aren't exactly religious, you may want to sigh and close the book at this point. However, this chapter is every inch as important as every other chapter that has been covered before. In this brief chapter, you will be exposed to your spiritual; self and shown how to make these principles work wonders for you.

Mindfulness and Mindfulness Practices for Increased Productivity

Mindfulness is a type of meditation in which one focuses on being acutely aware of their environment, what they are sensing and feeling right now, without seeking deeper meaning or subliminally judging their feelings. The aim of these practices is to relax the body and mind, reduce stress, and prime the mind for intense mental activity.

There are so many mindfulness practices you can try out today. However, here are just a few of them.

Self-Hypnosis

Self-hypnosis, although not considered to be a standard mindfulness practice, leans heavily on the practice of mindfulness to get into the deepest parts of the human mind to effect changes in behavior and one's reality.

As a matter of fact, many other mindfulness exercises you engage in will follow the same routine that was covered in Chapter 4 (on the subject of self-hypnosis and the detailed step-by-step process already covered in that chapter).

Start Every Day with Meditation

Once you roll out of bed in the morning, find a way to incorporate meditation into your daily morning routine. The good thing about meditation is that it gives you the space you need to concentrate, get your mind into gear, and just power up yourself for the day. Then again, the alertness and mental direction that comes from this will help you get through your day.

To-Do Lists Work Wonders

Before retiring to bed every night, take a few minutes to write out every single activity you would want to accomplish the next day. Arrange them in order of priority and attach timelines to them.

Throughout the night, your brain will mull over those activities, and you will find yourself waking up the next morning with the strength and fresh ideas to execute them. Then again, having your mind fixed on specific tasks reduces the chances that you'll veer off course the next day and start doing just about anything that comes to mind.

Do you want to increase your productivity dramatically? Maximize to-do lists.

Create a Distraction-Free Environment

This is where the lesson on decluttering (from Chapter 9) comes into play. When it is time for you to work and you can't just seem to get anything done, ensure you take out some time to figure out if the cause of your challenges isn't the distractions in your immediate environment.

Yoga

Yoga is a practice that stretches and engages both your mind and your body simultaneously. When used well, this routine can help you build your body strength even as you train your mind to be alert and ready for anything the day has for you. For the best results, invest your early hours in yoga as well. Then again, it doesn't have to run for hours. Even if all you can spare is just 30 minutes of your morning, you will start your day with positive energy, an alert mind, and a lithe body.

How to Make the Law of Attraction Work for You

The law of attraction is one of the fundamental laws of the universe. Simply put, the law of attraction teaches that anything you put your mind to will grow in and around you. It teaches that if you fill your mind with positive thoughts, positive results will be evident in your life. Conversely, if all you are preoccupied with are negative thoughts, you have to be ready to deal with the avalanche of negative things that will be happening to you.

Over the years, the law of attraction has been applied in various scenarios, and the results have been consistent. The results simply show that the law of attraction is real and not some juju that was made up by overbearing psychologists.

With these in place, here's how to make the law attraction work for you.

Know Exactly What You Want

If you don't know what you want (in every area of your life), you will end up attracting what you never thought you would. Most times, you would attract what you don't like.

Visualize Success

Do you remember the process we discussed in Chapter 4, where we talked about self-hypnosis? A time comes when you would have to add pictures to the entire process. This is where visualizing success comes in.

The more you visualize success, the more you send those signals into the atmosphere. As you keep doing this, the universe and all elements of nature will start aligning to give you what you want. It will only be a matter of time.

Affirmation and Gratitude

These go hand in glove. When you affirm, you speak what you want to see happening for you that day or year. Speaking was also a part of the self-hypnosis framework we discussed in Chapter 4 (so you now see that all these are interconnected, right?).

Gratitude, on the other hand, stems from mindfulness. It is the practice of teaching yourself how to always find the good in everything and continuously be grateful for the amazing things that are happening to you. Gratitude, when expressed with words, carries so much energy and can change your mood even for the rest of the day.

Start by practicing this. The next time you are about to get angry because of something, think of one good thing that has happened to you within the last 48 hours, say it aloud, and allow a huge smile to break out on your face. You will feel more energized to figure out a productive way out of the mess.

Keep Working Toward Your Goals

Visualization, affirmations, and all the mindfulness practices in the world will not get you success if you don't get off your behind and put in the work. An early chapter of this book covered goal setting and actualization in detail. You may want to revisit that section of the book and refresh your mind.

However, if you are able to combine all these mindfulness practices with the attitude of a go-getter, you may be amazed at the quality of results you would have after a few short years.

This is what makes a sigma male different from every other man around the block.

Chapter Summary

1. Spirituality isn't a concept you should wrinkle your face and frown at. It is simply the mechanism through which you

connect with your core, understand who you truly are, unleash your inner power, and own your genius.

2. The law of attraction is simple. Anything you give most of your time and attention to will eventually multiply in and around you. That is why there are a ton of mindfulness exercises you can engage in today to change the narrative around you. This chapter has covered a couple of them.

3. For the best results, pair all your mindfulness practices with cutting-edge goal-setting and goal-getting techniques. All the visualization in the world won't help you if you aren't keen on acting on the things that matter to you.

Conclusion

This book has covered what it means to be a sigma male. Over the course of the last 10 chapters, you have been held by the hand and taken through the world of extraordinary sigma males. You have been shown what it means to be a sigma male and also gained in-depth experience into what the world and life of a sigma male look like.

For the best results, you may want to skim through this book once again so that you can get a firmer hold of what has been discussed. Then again, this book is called "The Sigma Male Bible" for a reason because you may have to revert to it multiple times as you navigate through your everyday life. There is no point at which you would say you have read the book too many times. Every single time you hold this in your hands, you will learn something new that you can apply in your life immediately.

I sincerely hope that by reading this book, understanding and applying the concepts in it, and sticking things through until the end, you will tap into your superpower as a sigma male and see what it means to live a life that is beyond your wildest dreams; a life where everything is possible.

www.ingramcontent.com/pod-product-compliance
Lightning Source LLC
Chambersburg PA
CBHW070559100426
42744CB00006B/344